THE
VITAMIN
BOOK

THE VITAMIN BOOK

RICH WENTZLER

GRAMERCY PUBLISHING COMPANY
NEW YORK

Copyright © MCMLXXVIII by Rich Wentzler
All rights reserved.

This edition is published by Gramercy Publishing Company,
distributed by Crown Publishers, Inc.,
by arrangement with St. Martin's Press.

GRAMERCY 1980 EDITION

Manufactured in the United States of America

Library of Congress Cataloging in Publication Data

Wentzler, Rich.
　The vitamin book.

　Includes index.
　1. Vitamins in human nutrition. 2. Trace elements
in nutrition. I. Title.
QP 771W46　1980　612'.399　80-25442
ISBN 0-517-33409-7

k j i h

to Jim Parish
who got the ball rolling

Contents

Acknowledgements

This is the page that you usually skip because it lists all the people-you-never-heard-of who helped the writer out. Well, until I undertook this thing I had no idea how much help a person could need, or how generous people can be in providing it. People like Kathy Kalty, an overworked grad student who spent a healthy chunk of time copying references for me. Or Myron Seligman, who spent countless hours of his valuable time pumping biochemistry into me until his head began to hurt.

Or my father Lou, who snuck reams of manuscript through the office Xerox machine. And where would I have been without the New York Public Library, the Chemists' Club Library, or the library of the New York Academy of Medicine? Nowhere.

And then there were the people who answered silly questions with infinite patience; those who corrected, proofed and suggested through seemingly endless stacks of sloppy manuscript; and those who were just there when they were most needed: Ed Maisel, Mel Serio, Ruth Sackman of

Alternative Cancer Therapies, Charlotte Straus, Ernst Krebs, Al Berkenwald and my wife, Jennifer Yates.

These people gave of themselves with only one reward in mind—to see this book in print.

THE
VITAMIN
BOOK

The Vital Vitamins - an Introduction

Today medical science expects the average American to live to an age of just over seventy years. The near future will certainly see this figure take a dramatic jump, but there is no way of guessing from what we know now just how high it will go—because there is a revolution going on.

Every day seems to bring new discoveries from the controlled quiet of laboratories across the country. These discoveries point increasingly to a single glaring fact—that most of us have never known what it's like to be really healthy. For only now are we beginning to finally understand what fuels that most wonderful of machines—the human body.

And it is a machine, with more moving parts than there are grains of sand on earth. Any one of those moving parts might contain *millions* of active components. Every cell contains *billions* of important molecules and the body contains many *trillions* of cells. Now a billion alone is number enough to stagger the imagination. Suppose there is a carton that holds ten eggs. A hundred cartons fit into a box and a warehouse contains a thousand boxes. Imagine there are a thousand warehouses. Now count the eggs. That's a billion. And a trillion is a thousand billions.

The development of such a complex thing seems so unfathomable that one is tempted to say that God just lowered his magic wand and there we were. The truth may not be that simple, but it's much more interesting.

The first living things developed in the ocean and were just molecules that could duplicate themselves whenever their ingredients happened to be around. Today those things are called viruses, and they can find all the ingredients they need inside other living things, like you and me. The molecule was DNA and it just washed around in the ocean until it was lucky enough to land where there was . . . . well, food. It was rather like a tossed salad wandering in search of fresh chopped vegetables.

In those days that was all life was and there wasn't much to it . . . . until along swam a little creature with some built-in machinery for converting more common, everyday things into DNA. This fellow had the additional advantage of stowing his delicate DNA at the center of the machinery, where it was less exposed to the capricious turbulence of the outside world. The hitch was that the newcomer had to duplicate not only the DNA but all that machinery too. That was the price of being a cell.

Before long there were many different kinds of cells around, differing only in which common, everyday things they could duplicate themselves from. One group really had it made: they needed only water, a few minerals, carbon dioxide and sunshine. The first three they absorbed directly from the sea water around them, while for the fourth they had only to float at a shallow depth. This type of cell soon became fruitful and multiplied to fill the oceans (their descendants, algae and plankton, still do). They were the first plants.

Before plants could get too comfortable with their supremacy of the sea, another cell appeared that could manufacture copies of itself with only plant cells, oxygen and water for raw materials. It was the first animal. Other animals could do it by eating those animals, still others ate those, and some ate plants *and* animals, but all animals needed water and oxygen.

For a while there were experiments toward bigger and better cells, many equipped with elaborate gadgets for more efficiently getting the food to the cell and vice versa. When nature ran into some logistical problems in cells larger than half a millimeter or so, it shelved the problem for the moment (it remains unsolved) and tried a new tack. What it couldn't do with individual cells it achieved by *building* a king-sized creature out of many cells. This development gave rise to all sorts of interesting contraptions, including the most sophisticated yet, an example of which now reads this book. It also allowed the move from water to land, where many-celled plants used roots to extract water and minerals from the soil, and collected carbon dioxide and sunlight with leaves.

And, of course, when these cells got together they wound up building the one structure they knew best—they built a big cell, the whole in the image of the component. Roughly, our lungs, skin and intestines correspond to the cell's outer membrane (they determine what gets in and what goes out), our mouth and stomach to a cell's vacuoles and lysosomes, our brain to the cell's nucleus, and our blood to the sea water which surrounded those early cells.

By comparison with them, our problem is less one of reproduction than of fueling. Rather than have each of our trillions of cells duplicate themselves, then separate into two people, we simply produce tiny egg and sperm cells which can fuse into a "zygote". The zygote can grow into a new person all by itself, hopefully. This whole process is so efficient as to require only a small percentage of our food energy intake. The rest fuels the many gadgets with which the human body is equipped. Most of them, like our hands, legs, ears and eyes, originally served as food-finders for prehistoric man. Modern living has found other uses for them, but back then it was live to eat and eat to live, with no time for self-indulgence.

As the number of cells increased so did the possibilities for diversification. Different animals ate differently. If you've ever seen a dog gulp down large hunks of raw meat without chewing, you can guess that a dog's stomach is a little different from ours. The human stomach is specialized for the digestion of plants (vegetables, fruits, nuts, roots, berries, etc.), though we can also handle meat if it's been cooked enough; that is, partially digested by fire.

The ability of animals to use plants for fuel is based on a single fact: *all* forms of life are constructed from the same building blocks. There are basically three kinds of blocks— sugars, amino acids, and methyl groups. So what would *you* do if you wanted to make a church out of an out-house? Why take it apart, of course, and use the pieces to build anew.

Out of sugars you can build carbohydrates. You just chain them together like beads on a string. The really long chains are called starches. Sugars found in our food are fructose (the sweetest, found in fruits and honey), glucose and galactose. Sugar names end in "-ose". Table sugar (sucrose) is one molecule each of fructose and glucose hooked together.

Amino acids build proteins. There are over twenty different kinds, any number of which can be strung together any number of times; the chain can be many thousands of amino acids long. Protein names end with -in (or en or ine) and some familiar ones are hemoglobin, albumin, and gluten.

Fats are just strings of methyl (HCH) groups attached to an acetate molecule, if they're saturated. Unsaturated fats have some C (carbon) and CH groups thrown in. Liquid fats (oils) are less saturated than solid ones (butter, grease, lard, etc.).

The whole trick then is to break down the tissues of our food—be it wheat, watermelon, lamb, or grasshopper—and build human tissue out of the parts. In other words, you eat what you are.

This last is particularly true of proteins, which make up the actual machinery of life, while carbohydrates and fats serve as the fuel for that machinery. Thus if the body was a car, protein would be the car itself, carbohydrate the gasoline and fat the spare can in the trunk. Which ties a pretty ribbon around a neat, greatly simplified package that represented the state of our understanding of nutrition at the turn of the century. If only life were as perfect as the tidy picture scientists painted of it in those days. In truth, the people had a brief life expectancy and suffered from countless miseries, many of which are just memories today; like rickets, scurvy, beriberi and pellagra.

The doctors started with searches for the "germs" that caused these diseases. That they were unsuccessful is perhaps an encouraging sign. If man really was subject to rampant attacks by so many different microbes, he would seem a pretty weak sister to the rest of the animal kingdom, all of whom, by comparison, are rarely sick.

Rather, the victims of those diseases were found to have broken, unknowingly, a nutritional rule—something a free-living animal would not, in fact *could* not, do. All nutritional rules basically reduce to a single maxim: No creature shall part company with the environment that formed it. The first evidence of this came when experiments showed that animals fed rich diets of pure protein, carbohydrate, and fat inevitably grew ill and died. Clearly there were any number of vital substances in food that would all have to be identified before there was any thought of feeding humans a "test tube dinner". And yet at that very moment a trend was underway aimed at achieving exactly that. The best example of it is seen in the sad history of bread.

Wheat is a hardy little plant that bids fair to nudge out Rover for the honor of being man's best friend. It soaks up sunshine all summer long, converting it into fuel. Like any expectant parent, it sets aside a portion of its hard-earned wealth for junior. Come September, the plant produces seeds. Since these seeds will have to make it in the world unaided, each one is provided with a coat that gram for gram is one of the richest sources of nutrients known. One might compare it with milk, for plant-babies. All this men have known for thousands of years. Accordingly, they gathered up the coated seeds ("grains"), ground them into flour, and made many nutritious things of it, most notably bread. What they didn't know was that the nutrients in the grain are *not* uniformly distributed throughout it. The same is true of an apple. In both cases the essential vitamins and amino acids are found in two places—the core and just under the skin. In wheat the core (where the seed is) is called the germ and the skin called bran. The germ and bran together contain more nutrients than any other natural source. In between is carbohydrate, about as pure and nutritionally worthless as water. Guess which part goes into our bread.

Somewhere along the line an idea crept into the mind of a flour-miller as he watched the brown germ and bran separate from the heavier (but lighter in color) starch, that perhaps he could improve the bread by removing one or the other fractions. Unfortunately for all of us, he guessed wrong. A meaningless psychological preference for things white over things brown seems to pervade many aspects of our lives. It may be related to dislike for an unpalatable brown substance with which we all deal on a daily basis, and the desire to be clean. Whatever the reason, this innate prejudice has caused our species many setbacks, the most serious of which, after racism, is our collective abandonment of brown bread, rice, and sugar for white.

At present over a dozen substances that are essential to our survival are known to exist in that original wheat grain. A dozen more are suspected and the search for still more continues. Most of these are lumped together as the "B complex". Others are called "unsaturated fatty acids" (sometimes known as vitamin F). When the wheat grain arrives at the mill it contains all of these, along with vitamins E and, indirectly, A. When what remains of the grain emerges, few are left. An attempt to "enrich" bread by replacing some of the B_1, B_2, and B_3 is probably of no real value at all, as will be seen.

The blame for this crime usually falls on industry, but they are at most only half responsible; for industries exist only so long as they fill the wants of their customers. If there weren't millions of willing consumers pouring into the stores each day to buy it, this worse-than-useless (thanks to bleaches, emulsifiers, preservatives, and other harmful additives) bread would never be made. When you buy a product, you support it.

Every cell in your body (population: trillions) requires

vitamins every single day. What exactly makes them so essential is something we are only now beginning to understand. For each vitamin the story is different, since each acts in its own way. Many, however, share one common property.

The body is a machine in which the moving parts are chemicals. All of the trillions of events that occur in the body every second, even during sleep, are chemical reactions changing one chemical to another. The time it takes for a reaction to happen varies with the reaction. Some occur in the blink of an eye, others are not so fast.

Take, for example, the oxidation of paper. If you sat and watched a piece of paper for about twenty years, you would begin to notice the edges turning yellowish. This is because oxygen is reacting with the paper to produce carbon dioxide and ash. Keep watching that paper and you'll find it has turned to black dust after a few thousand years. If you wanted to make ash and you had paper, oxygen, and a few thousand years to wait, that's one way you could get it. But if you're less patient, you'll *catalyze* the reaction—that is, speed it up—by setting a match to it.

If you sat down to breakfast and had to wait for each of the thousands of slow-poke reactions—eye to nerve, nerve to brain, brain to another nerve, nerve to hand muscle and so on—you'd starve to death before the spoon ever reached your mouth. So the body controls and catalyzes all those reactions with chemicals called enzymes.

Most of the body's thousands of enzymes it makes itself, for they are extremely complicated and fragile molecules that must frequently be replaced. This isn't necessary in every case however, because large pieces of some important enzymes can be found in food. The body just has to make the adjoining piece and hook it up with the piece from the food to make the complete enzyme, saving itself the trouble of manufacturing the whole thing. The piece that comes from food is called a co-enzyme and that's what most of the B-vitamins are—co-enzymes.

Other vitamins, anti-oxidants, stand guard against damage to key molecules in the body. Still others act like hormones, which control growth, sexuality, metabolism, etc. Most of the minerals are involved in activation of enzymes and vitamins: rather like the little ignition key of a big automobile—it may be small but without it the car is useless.

In most cases we know what happens when someone does completely without a vitamin, and the results are grisly. What is less clear is the effect of a long period of not getting quite enough, and that's what many of us are doing today. It may only be coincidence, but *never*, before this century, was heart disease such a killer. When we hear that so-and-so "died of a heart attack", we rarely realize that such attacks can only be the result of years of ill health and heart trouble. We have come to think of heart attacks as a "natural" way to die. That's how common heart disease is. Cancer was a fairly rare condition until the last hundred years or so. Animals seldom get it, even when they live in our homes. Never has history seen so many in search of help for "mental" problems, most of which are symptoms of nervous system disorders. And, the common cold has never been commoner.

Again, it may be only coincidence. Yet vitamins and minerals are known to play key roles in all of the above health problems. Consider Denmark's experience during World War I. For economic reasons the refining of flour stopped and the people ate whole wheat bread. After the war refining was resumed. Looking back over the figures many years later, statisticians found that cancer, heart and kidney disease, diabetes, and the overall death rate had all taken dramatic drops during the war. Coincidence? Maybe, but these same conditions are markedly increased in animals deprived of one or more vitamins.

Facts like these have leaked through a curtain of misinformation to spark a movement in this country that may, before it's finished, bring about untold improvement in the quality and enjoyability of our lives through the priming of our bodies. A direct consequence of this movement, however, has been the recent flood of "mega-vitamin" therapies; taking massive doses of a vitamin on the philosophy that you can't get too much of a good thing. The benefits of these therapies vary from person to person and from vitamin to vitamin. Some are useful, some a waste of time, and others downright dangerous.

To untangle conflicts like these we must examine each of these nutrients separately, to discover how they work their wonders.

Vitamin A

If there were a runner-up award for the most popular color among plants, the winner would be orange. Think of apricots, cantaloupe, squash, marigolds, yams, mangoes, and, of course, oranges. What all these plants have in common is a group of colorful chemicals called carotenes, named after carrots. Carotenes run the color range from yellow (peaches) to red (tomatoes) and occur in almost every plant.

Carotenes also occur in the people who eat plants. So as long as these chemicals are going to be floating around inside us anyway, the body decided to put them to work. It found a way to convert one of the carotenes (beta-carotene) into something else and gave the new chemical some important jobs to do. It was vitamin A.

The first of these jobs to be discovered is done in the eye. When the eye sees there are actually two different kinds of vision occurring at once. For each kind there is a special cell in the retina, both named for shapes they resemble. Cone cells respond to colors and require a lot of light to do so. Rod cells, on the other hand, are not color-sensitive, but are able to function even in very dark surroundings.

11

It's the rod cells that especially depend on vitamin A . . . . sort of. Actually vitamin A itself doesn't really do anything. The body converts it to one of three slightly different chemicals depending on the job at hand. It can be either vitamin A aldehyde, vitamin A acid, or vitamin A palmitate. Rod cells use the aldehyde.

Inside the rods are thousands of little discs packed with vitamin A aldehyde molecules, each one hooked to a protein. When a light particle strikes one of these pairs, it splits it. The liberated vitamin A wakes up some calcium ions which in turn go over and ring the bell. The "bell" is a direct nerve-line to the brain. The number of calcium ions that ring it tells the brain how much light is falling on that particular rod cells. When every rod cell is heard from, the brain can put together a black-and-white photograph of what we're looking at, with rod cells as the individual grains. Cone cells, if there's light enough, paint the picture with color and that's how we see.

Since this process occurs many times a second for most of every day, some of the vitamin A aldehyde molecules are bound to get broken. So the body makes replacements out of vitamin A, but it can't do that unless it gets enough from food. Without it, rod cells begin to deteriorate, causing night blindness—inability to see in the dark. This is the first symptom of vitamin A deficiency and studies have shown that as many as a *third* of all Americans suffer from it. The most serious consequence of this is auto accidents, which occur most often in relative darkness. The problem is cleared up quickly by more vitamin A, but further deficiency will cause complete and permanent damage to the retina, resulting in blindness. In impoverished areas of the world, vitamin A deficiency is the leading cause of blindness.

Another job that requires vitamin A aldehyde is sperm production. Deficiency of vitamin A eventually causes impotence, which is easily cured by increased A. In alcoholics things are more complicated; an alcoholic can become impotent no matter how much vitamin A he gets. This is because the conversion of vitamin A to vitamin A aldehyde uses the same enzyme that breaks down alcohol. Vitamin A loses out in the competition for that enzyme, since the body cannot allow potentially fatal alcohol poisoning. But vision and sex together account for less than 5% of our vitamin A use.

Surrounding the cell and each tiny organ inside it are thin wrappers called membranes. They are the cell's customs' officials; they decide what goes in and what goes out, what stays in and what stays out. To keep its membranes in good working order, the cell needs just the right amount of vitamin A. Too much makes the membrane brittle, too little makes it overly flexible; in both cases the membrane malfunctions, allowing the bad molecules to sneak in and the good ones to leak out.

This becomes especially serious where lysosomes are concerned. The lysosome is like a portable stomach, a small bubble that floats around in the protoplasm looking for food. Inside it are enzymes that can digest just about anything organic. When food enters the cell, it is surrounded by another bubble called a vacuole. When the vacuole bumps into the lysosome, the two bubbles merge, whereupon the enzymes attack and digest the food. If the membrane is getting either too little or too much vitamin A, some of the enzymes can escape from the lysosome and begin digesting the cell. This is not good. In fact it is such an effective way of killing cells that large doses of vitamin A are being pumped into tumors to increase the effect of X-ray and

chemotherapy treatments in knocking off cancer cells. Lysosomes once seemed such an all-around hazard to health that
some scientists guessed their function was providing quick
relief for cells that grew tired of living. Science has come a
long way.

We can now guess just what it is about vitamin A that
lets it do the things it does.

For the most part the body's components mesh together
with amazing harmony. Every molecule has a job to do and
they don't get in each other's way . . . . for the most part. One
of the more obnoxious exceptions is a molecule delinquent
called the free radical. Free radicals all have the same
problem—one electron too many. So they wander around
the cell looking for a place to dump their extra electron. If
one succeeds in unloading it on an unsuspecting membrane
molecule, the result will be damage—a tiny hole poked into
the membrane. Enough of these punctures will make the
membrane useless. This whole process of electron donation
is called oxidation, and vitamin A is an anti-oxidant.

Vitamin A is specially designed to scavenge free radicals
from membranes. The radicals prefer attacking vitamin A
to membranes, which are preserved at the vitamin's expense. To enable the vitamin to do this properly, it was
given the ability to mesh smoothly and easily into the heart
of the membrane. But you have to remember that vitamin
A is not membrane material. If you send too much in there
you won't have any free radical damage but you won't have
any membrane either.

But even free radicals have been put to work in some of
the body's processes, and vitamin A must always be on the
spot to keep them from getting out of hand. For example,
when a skin cell dies it is replaced by special cells that lie
beneath it, like spare teeth. For skin cells *inside* the body

(the linings of our stomachs, throats, lungs and nasal passages) this gets a little complicated because there are two different kinds of cell. One of them produces mucus, to keep those areas moist and well-lubricated, and the other has little hairs that keep the mucus moving, so it doesn't clog things up. Now if a cell of either type should die, the spare cell underneath can replace it by becoming a cell of the same type. The thing that makes one cell different from another is the kind of protein it makes. The blueprint the cell uses for building protein is RNA. The blueprint for RNA is DNA. The manufacture of DNA is regulated by cyclic AMP, whose manufacture is in turn regulated by *prostaglandins*. And prostaglandins are made by a free radical reaction.

That's how vitamin A can affect your skin. If there were not enough A, your mucus cells would die without being replaced. The result is dry, rough, itching, scaling skin along with pimples, soreness of the eyes, and proneness to infection. For this reason the vitamin is being used successfully to treat acne, psoriasis, and several other skin conditions, most of them rare. Thus far the best technique seems to be direct application of vitamin A acid to the affected area. If you think you might benefit from it, see your doctor.

It's no coincidence that a large percentage of cancers arise in mucus tissues. If a cancer-causing agent is going to get at us, it must come either through the air we breathe, the things we touch or the food we eat; hence the profusion of lung, skin and digestive tract cancers. The ability of some chemicals to cause cancer depends on free radicals inside the cell to change it to a chemical that *really* causes cancer. Vitamin A, in preventing that conversion, can nip tumor development in the bud. But the link between cancer and vitamin A doesn't end there.

This versatile vitamin has been shown to discourage tumor development, inhibit tumor growth and speed tumor destruction in *all* parts of the body. This applies not only to both chemical and virus-caused tumors, but to those directly transplanted into test animals. It may be significant here that cancer cells themselves aren't very interested in vitamin A and don't ordinarily ingest it.

These facts illustrate the importance of diet in avoiding and treating cancer, a relationship that is strengthened by research in every passing year. In any event, vitamin A certainly does not act alone in this regard. For most of its tasks it must share the responsibility with other vitamins (D, C, E and K), and hormones.

In fact, vitamin A acts very much like a hormone itself. Like the sex hormones, vitamin A can determine how a cell "grows up", and like all hormones it works directly on the glands that make and distribute other hormones, regulating them somehow. What distinguishes A from the hormones is that, instead of coming from a gland, vitamin A is secreted by the refrigerator.

One of A's spheres of influence is the intense hormone factory located inside the adrenal glands. The outsides of these glands make a special hormone, adrenalin, but the cortex makes a whole hormone family, most notably cortisone. Cortisone (named after the cortex) and the other cortical hormones are all made from cholesterol. That's why vitamin A can, by raising the levels of these steroid hormones, lower blood cholesterol.

Vitamin A also participates in the detoxification of many poisons, including sodium nitrite and nitrate. Of course no one would knowingly consume these poisons—yet they are added to virtually all packaged meats. Check the ingredients.

As for growth, about all we can say for sure is that babies who do not get enough vitamin A in the crucial year or so following conception are subject to about every gruesome deformity you can think of. But the same is true if they get too much, so knowing how to get the right amount is important.

Vitamin A is found in nature only where animals store it—mostly in the liver, some in the kidneys, and traces in fat tissue, through which it trickles into egg yolks, cream and unwashed butter. But the best way to get vitamin A is not to eat it, but to make it yourself, from beta-carotene. A beta-carotene molecule is rather like two vitamin A molecules with their tails tied together. Our small intestine contains an enzyme that chops the knot and liberates vitamin A.

Beta-carotene is orange and can be found in fruits and vegetables of the red-orange-yellow range, but it also occurs wherever there is chlorophyll, the green pigment. So the leaves of green plants are also rich sources of vitamin A. Beta-carotene is a somewhat hardier chemical than vitamin A, but is still quite delicate. Heat, light and exposure to oxygen are the things that destroy it, and the effect of these things is proportional to the amount of them and the length of time they operate. Storage, ideally, should be moist, cold, dark, airtight and as short as possible. Cooking should be at a minimum temperature for a minimal length of time, covered to keep out air and light. If you throw out the cooking water, beta-carotene will go with it. But even if you get this far successfully, the struggle isn't necessarily over.

Vitamin A dissolves in oil, not water, and must be dissolved for the intestinal wall to absorb it. This means that your diet must contain a certain amount of fat or oil. But the enzymes in our digestive tract are water-soluble, and, as we all know, oil and water don't mix. So the body supplies a chemical that breaks down the oil into tiny droplets, a process called emulsification. Without it, vitamin A could hide at the center of large oil drops where enzymes couldn't get at it. We run into the same problem when trying to wash away fat and grease. It won't dissolve in water so we use an emulsifier called soap to break it into small particles that are easily rinsed away.

The body's emulsifier is bile, which is pumped into the digestive tract by the liver. Many liver disorders can result in vitamin A loss through insufficient bile production. But thanks to some of the "miracles" of modern technology, we may be in as great a danger of the opposite, but equally serious problem.

About forty years ago food industry researchers—in search of a softer, fluffier bread and a smoother, creamier peanut butter—began adding artificial emulsifiers to our groceries. The problem was that the emulsifiers, having already done their job by pleasing our senses of sight and touch, would have to be eaten, since there is no way of getting them out. The problem with these superfluous additives is that they can cause excessive A absorption and its many unpleasant consequences.

In 1975 an Englishman named Basil Brown, either scornful or unaware of those consequences, was certain he had found in vitamin A the key to perfect health. Mr. Brown began taking seven million units (roughly a thousand times the recommended dose) and drinking a gallon of carrot juice a day. How was he two weeks later?

Dead. At the age of 48.

The cause was found to be complete destruction of the liver—cirrhosis. His skin was bright yellow when he died.

Incidents like this have pressured the Food and Drug

Administration into making dosages over 10,000 IU per tablet illegal without prescription. But this ruling has at most psychological value inasmuch as it cannot regulate the number of tablets one takes. Toxic amounts are estimated at around 200,000 IU daily, or a single dose of two million IU. For infants, divide by ten. Quantities like this cannot come from food, unless you eat the liver of an animal that eats lots of liver. An ounce of polar bear liver has enough A to kill thirty rats. But aside from this the only way to poison yourself is with the use of supplements.

Most multivitamins contain the average Recommended Daily Allowance of 5,000 IU, in the form of synthetic vitamin A palmitate. Conversion of vitamin A to palmitate is the first thing the body does with it before shipping it off to the liver for storage, so taking palmitate theoretically saves the body some work. Separate vitamin A supplements are usually palmitate too, often with an oil added to ensure absorption. Also available is pre-emulsified vitamin A to save the body more "work". This may be useful in cases of diarrhea or acute illness, but it should be remembered that a "working" body is the definition of good health. "Organic" A is an extract of fish liver oil and is pure vitamin A (the alcohol form, also called retinol). Synthetic vitamin A acetate is also on the market and has no advantages over the others. Something called vitamin A_2, in the unlikely event you should run across it, is almost identical to vitamin A in structure but only half as effective in your body.

For those in good health, vitamin A supplements cannot be recommended. Consider for instance that someone who gets the best amount from his food *and* takes a supplement will be getting *more* than the best amount, which cannot be the best amount. Conversely, if the supplement has the best amount, one is faced with the awkward problem of *avoiding*

vitamin A in food! This is why beta-carotene was earlier
suggested as the best source of vitamin A. The advantage is
that the body is able to control the conversion of beta-
carotene in accordance with its needs. Thus Mr. Brown's
carrot juice alone would not have harmed him. His body
would have shut off the conversion process after it had what
it needed. Over vitamin A, however, the body has no control, it must absorb what we eat. All this suggests that we
are better equipped to handle vitamin A from plant than
from animal and chemical sources. This last will be doubly
important until science determines just how much A we
should get.

Until then we can only read the Recommended Daily Allowances for the U.S. (higher than those of most countries)
and bear in mind some general facts. Men generally need
more A than women and adults more than children. Requirements increase with body weight and we use more in
winter than in summer. Intoxication and illness, especially
hepatitis and pneumonia, can deplete our liver reserves of
A, so convalescents will need more. So will diabetics and
those with over-active thyroids. Long-term exposure to
harsh lighting conditions will speed up a destruction in the
eye, raising requirements.

And then there are vitamin A destroyers. Mineral oil, a
common laxative, cannot be emulsified and will gobble up
all your A. Tannic acid from tea, nitrates and benzoate from
polluted water and preserved food, an iron supplement
called ferrous sulfate, and citral, an artificial lemon flavor-
ing, all destroy vitamin A. So do aspirin and barbiturates.

The air we breathe daily brings us in contact with dozens
of deadly pollutants that don't do us more damage because
they are busy destroying vitamin A in the lungs. Persons
who breathe polluted air need more A. But all these things

your body knows already and can deal with by itself if it gets plenty of carotene.

Deficiencies of A can be caused by other deficiencies. Vitamin E, another anti-oxidant, will sacrifice itself to protect vitamin A in storage. Zinc, it seems, is absolutely essential for proper use and storage of A. Adding zinc to vitamin A supplements seems like a good idea.

Every cell in the body needs vitamin A and to reach them all it must get around. It does so via the blood stream, a route traveled by traffic of all shapes and sizes. On this route vitamin A has its own private car and won't travel in anything else. This car is made up entirely of protein, to which vitamin A can attach or detach itself. The point is that without this protein the vitamin will be left waiting at the station, soon to pass through to excretion. In this way lack of protein, as with vitamin E and zinc, causes vitamin A deficiency and to avoid it one needs both a good quantity and a good variety of protein.

Following is a list of vitamin A and carotene-rich foods, with a table of current RDAs. Bear in mind that an IU (international unit) is about half a millionth of a gram. Because of the arbitrary nature of this unit, popularity is growing for another: 1 RE (retinol equivalent) = 1 μg vitamin A = 6 μg beta-carotene = 12 μg of other carotenes. 1 μg (microgram) = a millionth of a gram.

Food vitamin concentrations are essential to us if we're to have any idea where we stand nutritionally, but they're as hard to come by as they are necessary. Chemistry's traditional analytical methods have generally proven fruitless when working with these hypersensitive molecules. Deprived of the tried and true, biochemists have dreamt up many ingenious, elaborate and original, but necessarily indirect, ways of counting vitamins. And this makes for fascinating, but necessarily unreliable numbers.

To make matters worse, every eggplant has a vitamin content that's as unique to it as your personality is to you, depending on who that eggplant's parents were, what diseases it was exposed to, how many weeds and other eggplants it had to compete with for eggplant essentials, innumerable other factors, and that's only the beginning. Then comes the point in its life-cycle at which it was harvested, how long it's spent moping around in trucks, grocery stores, refrigerators, etc. and at what temperatures, and of course the hundreds of ways a person might cook it.

After all this it seems silly to say anything as blithely general as "eggplants have more vitamins than mushrooms". Yet that's what we're doing. If you allow for all the guesswork though, you may find these tables a useful crutch on the road to better health. Just don't lean on them too heavily.

Since grains and beans are cooked at such varying dilutions, they're given in the raw, dry form. Vegetables too are raw, while meats are lightly cooked. The table tells you how much you can hope for from a food; how much you get is up to you. All values are weight-standardized to 100 grams, or a bit less than a quarter (0.220) of a pound. Well, so much for the appetizers—Let's have some food.

International Units/100 grams Vitamin A			
mushrooms	0	salmon	300
eggwhite	0	walnuts	300
white grapefruit	10	plums	300
sprouts	15	oysters	310
pears	20	summer squash	400
beets	20	green peppers	420
sesame seeds	30	tangerines	420
sardines	30	pink grapefruit	440
olives	33	mackerel	450
piñon nuts	38	okra	520
sunflower seeds	50	mature sprouts	550
shrimp	50	watermelon	590
chickpeas	50	kumquats	600
lentils	58	soybeans	700
cauliflower	60	halibut	850
strawberries	60	asparagus	900
bluefish	62	tomatoes	900
yogurt	70	lobster	920
pineapple	70	cream	1000
tuna	80	lettuce	1000
apples	90	cherries	1000
rhubarb	100	eggs	1200
blueberries	100	cheeses	1300
cashews	100	peaches	1300
grapes	100	pitangas	1500
bass	100	pumpkin	1600
soy lecithin	100	eel	1600
clams	100	nectarines	1600
hazelnuts	110	papayas	1700
cow milk	125	mangoes	1800
raspberries	130	romaine	1900
pecans	130	whitefish	2000
cabbage	130	swordfish	2100
avocados	150	crab	2200
artichoke	150	pimentoes	2300
herring	150	broccoli	2500
cod	170	apricots	2700
oranges	200	persimmons	2700
pistachios	230	endive	3300
human milk	240	cantaloupe	3400
cucumbers	250	egg yolk	3400
guava	280	winter squash	4000

red peppers	4400	carrots	11000	
watercress	5000	dandelion greens	14000	
chard	6500	calve's liver	22000	
collard greens	6500	cow liver	44000	
spinach	8100	sheep liver	45000	
turnip greens	8500	red palm oil	90000	
parsley	8500	cod liver oil	200,000	
kale	8900	shark liver oil	12,000,000	
yams	9000	polar bear liver	50,000,000	

Recommended Daily Allowances
for Vitamin A

birth - 6 months	1400 IU
6 months - 1 year	2000 IU
1 - 3 years	2000 IU
4 - 6 years	2500 IU
7 - 10 years	3500 IU
11+ years	5000 IU (men) 4000 IU (women)
pregnant women	5000 IU
lactating women	6000 IU

The B Complex

After losing a tennis match or a game of chess you can always try again, maybe with someone easier. But in the game of natural selection your opponent is always Death, and if you don't win you can't play. The game is rough, and there are many more losers than survivors. To be born is to find oneself in an arena.

To find out what it takes to get ahead in this free-for-all slug-out one need only pick up the clues left in the evolutionary history of life on this planet—the species that are still around today represent the best nature has come up with yet in the survival department.

But even nature's best work won't be left alone. Forces have been in action since the dawn of life, inexorably adjusting the organism's master blueprint, the DNA molecule. Each tiny change in that molecule means a change in the organism, a new creature created. These struggling neophytes are then greeted with the cruelest of tests—the fight for life—which only one in a million will survive. The vast majority of such mutations are hopeless deformities, created by a force which acts without rhyme or reason, and the individuals are doomed to be crowded out of the food supply long before they reach the age of reproduction. It's not surprising that one mutation in a million often has an improved way of dealing with food, either of getting or of using it.

But this whole chain of thought runs into a contradiction when it comes to co-enzymes: here it seems that somebody struggled through to success not because of a new ability, but because of a *lack* of one.

An important clue is that while plants usually make their own co-enzymes, animals rarely do. Apparently there were once two types of animals living at the same time (a very early one on the evolutionary scale) and in the same environment, but with one basic difference. While one could manufacture all the co-enzymes it needed, the other was born without the necessary molecular machinery. That difference really shouldn't have been terribly important since both were eating things rich in the contested co-enzymes. But it was important enough to make one of those primitive predecessors extinct, and to this day its example has never been followed. Maybe making things that are already plentiful in food is just too much of a waste.

And co-enzymes *are* plentiful—considering that all food is or was a living thing; and it wouldn't have been alive if it was short of co-enzymes. The richest plant sources are the parts that do the most living; the seeds, growing sprouts, and leaves. The richest animal sources are organs that store eaten co-enzymes (most often the liver). When the whole co-enzyme collection is found in special abundance it's called the B complex. That's because they decided to name the vitamins in alphabetical order as they discovered them, and what was first called vitamin B turned out to be a bit more complex. To date, well over a dozen things have been isolated from it. Some of those aren't co-enzymes at all, but people who don't eat them die. Others are co-enzymes all right, but without them people get along fine. There is one thing, though, that all the B vitamins have in common: they take to water.

If you're in the body and you're in a hurry, water is the way to go. In effect, water is the handle by which things are carried from one part of the body to another. The heart is able to grip this handle by virtue of water's amazing hydraulic properties. So if the heart pumps water somewhere the things dissolved in it will tag right along. If the thing to be moved doesn't happen to dissolve in water the body goes back to the drawing board.

But all the B vitamins dissolve in water just fine. In fact, they're the only ones that do (except vitamin C, which is anomalous in more ways than one). This advantage, however, can also work the other way.

The problem is that the body also uses water to wash the bugs out of its intricate works. It does this by pumping whole blood down toward the bladder while giving the kidneys a chance to pluck out all the things it thinks the body ought to hang onto—like red cells, minerals and B vitamins—and allowing the rest to leave us as urine. But the kidney can't catch everything, so even under the best of circumstances we flush away a few B vitamins every day. And in the body, as in so much of this wonderful world of ours, circumstances are rarely at their best.

Not surprisingly, anything that increases the amount of water we excrete likewise increases the B vitamin content of the toilet. And in our present way of life, that anything includes just about everything. Examples include aspirin, alcohol, amphetamine, caffeine, nicotine, marijuana, tranquilizers, food coloring, narcotics, antihistamines, even (when taken in large amounts) vitamin C, protein, B vitamins, and, of course, water itself.

So—just like the speed freaks, alcoholics, mariholics and junkies—people using liquid diets against a virus or diarrhea, others undergoing diuretic therapy, and those who just prefer drinking to eating; *all* are raising their own B vitamin requirements. This is a fact that should be weighed against the benefits, whether for health or esthetics, of such common practices. And the same goes for anyone experimenting with the new-fashioned mega-vitamin dosages of vitamin C or the vitamins B. Said self-made guinea pig assures himself sufficient quantities of one vitamin at the risk of developing deficiencies in all the rest.

Naturally the question is always how much we need and solutions are always in short supply. The FDA's RDAs, for instance, vary all the time, depending on what exciting new testing method they've come up with. It's not comforting to know that the amount that's right today will be too much or too little tomorrow.

With the B vitamins we have some freedom of choice: when we get tired of worrying about "how much?" we can worry about "in what proportions?"—because there are times when co-enzymes, like many of nature's children, come to need one another. In this case it's a working relationship.

It all starts when the body needs to convert one molecule to another. Of course it would be nice if all the body's key reactions could take place in a single magical moment, but reality finds the magic spread among a series of steps, each attended by its own enzyme. The system is, in effect, an assembly line, with the raw materials going in at one end and the finished products exiting at the other. Between lies an array of specialized workers, each of whom has a job that begins where the last fellow left off and ends where the next takes up, and none of whom can be replaced by another type of enzyme. Every step of the process brings the original molecule that much closer to being the desired one.

Now an enzyme, like any other worker, needs his tools, and that's where co-enzymes come in: if there's a shortage of a certain co-enzyme the enzyme that needs it might as well not show up for work. And it takes only one absentee to bring the whole system to a grinding halt which no amount of other co-enzymes can revive. So what's needed here is not so much the individual B vitamins but the whole assembly line, in other words, co-enzymes in the same *proportions* found in nature. In cases where the job happens to be small enough for a single enzyme to handle, this least-common-denominator problem is avoided altogether. It then becomes a question of how much of the necessary co-enzyme should be supplied to best do the job.

Suppose you had a roomful of potato peelers peeling potatoes. If everybody has a knife then everything's fine. A few extras are okay, maybe even a lot, but when some maniac in the Supply Dept. has the room filling up with knives, burying potato and peeler alike, it's too much already.

It's the kidney's responsibility to prevent this sort of thing, but the excess co-enzymes excreted inevitably drag along others that were just minding their own business—a sad waste of the kidney's time and energy, and of vitamins too. The moral is that larger amounts are better amounts only if the body really needs them.

You might think that the liver should take advantage of having extra B vitamins around and tuck some away for a rainy day. In fact though, that question was taken up long, long ago and today they aren't stored. The idea was that since all food (being life) is rich in co-enzymes, why bother? But that was long, long ago when the miracles of modern technology were still undreamed of. Since then, food has descended from the central essential of life to just another of the ever-increasing number of ways to please the senses. The meal which once was a tentative daily renewal on the contract of life is now a routine formality, expected to provide relief from the greatest of all evils—boredom.

To this end the appearance and flavor of a product like Wonder Bread are shaped to fit the personality created for it by advertising. Since man has only his senses to follow, the traps are laid accordingly. Exotic wrappers mimic the colors of the original unfortunate plant or animal, long since departed from this earth. The sweet tooth that once guided man to the ripest (and most nutritious) fruits on the tree, now leads him to the candy aisle.

Lost in the shuffle are the humble B vitamins, which can neither be seen nor tasted.

Freezing, for instance, allows us to eat foods that are no longer fresh. Besides a loss of flavor, they also offer one-third fewer Bs. Canning is twice as bad.

The wheat berry is a tough nut to crack, and to pulverize it a lot of power is required. If you're not careful though, your milling machine will get very hot, hot enough to scorch some 12% of your Bs to a frazzle. Being careful! means using stone grinders. What happens next isn't a matter of care; it's a simple case of institutionalized idiocy.

The germ and bran are removed and fed to pigs and cattle, none of whom develop cancer, schizophrenia, or heart disease. Although only around 30% of the wheat is lost in this way, it happens to be the cream of the crop. By the time the "wheat" flour is bleached, baked, shipped, and shelved maybe 10% of the B complex survives.

Under government pressure the food industry replaced three of the cheapest vitamins (a loaf's worth of B_3 "enrichment" costs well under a hundredth of a cent) and passed what expense there was along to the consumer, who likewise foots the bill for removing them in the first place. Here, as usual, half an effort turns out to be worse than none at all—for this feeble gesture shatters whatever balance remained in the refined grain, thus disturbing the body's ability to handle B vitamins from other sources.

But it's the very absurdity of this state of affairs that gives reason for hope. Facts like these just won't stand the light of day much longer. In the meantime studies indicate that easily half the people in this country are suffering from at least one of the wide spectrum of deficiency diseases associated with the B complex.

There are, of course, separate diseases for the separate vitamins, becoming more and more distinct as the body gets less and less of the vitamin in question. But most often the diseases exist simultaneously, mildly and well blended with one another. As time goes on the balance may tip back and forth, favoring first one deficiency then another, as the sufferer alters his vitamin intake, protein/fat/carbohydrate ratios or energy output. The result is a constantly shifting cluster of symptoms that can vary widely with the widely varying ways that people are put together. In general though, the signs of B deficiencies are most noticeable in two areas.

First is the nervous system because, being the thing that does our noticing for us, it notices itself first. The clues may come in the form of impatience, depression, or confusion, later developing into hallucinations, panic, or complete withdrawal as neurosis becomes psychosis. It's unfortunate that the early signs are often considered normal human behavior, something one should learn to accept both in oneself and in others. Better nutrition offers hope for a brighter world.

Second is the skin, because it's the part of us with which two important senses, sight and touch, are most intimate. The changes begin as local dryness, itching, and scaling, eventually becoming sores. Especially prone to these symptoms is the mouth area, including the lips and tongue.

In fact an elaborate if imprecise system has been worked out that attempts to pin down exactly which B is deficient, depending on whether the rash develops on your elbow or your wrist, your lip or the corner of your mouth, whether your tongue turns scarlet or purple. But even if such information could be trusted it would be unwise to use it in any but the most extreme situations—because the B vitamins are almost always found together in food, so anyone not getting enough of one is probably missing others as well. The answer then is to treat all such cases with the whole complex.

Getting the B complex in food isn't as easy as it once was or will, before long, be. It's a sad comment on the quality of our food processing when the most nutritious meals are those which come in contact with it least. Thus it seems wiser to humbly forego those foods most blessed with the touch of technology, and to get to your food before the processors do. You have to stay pretty close to the source.

Animal foods are quite rich in B vitamins considering that the animals they come from are essentially unable to make any. The Bs get from the plant to the animal kingdom via animals that eat plants and animals that eat plant-eating animals. And, since there isn't much the digestive tract likes better to pull out of food than B vitamins, they reach a higher concentration in animals than in plants; especially in the liver, the enzyme crossroads of the body. In fact, such is the concentration that in spite of the extensive processing meat undergoes, its B levels are still pretty respectable, especially in the organ meats—liver, kidney, heart, and brain. Plants themselves concentrate their Bs in the leaves, seeds, nuts, and grains.

How many of those vitamins actually make it to your stomach though, depends on how fresh they are and how much abuse they've sustained *en route*. Cooking heat and cooking time should be kept minimal, and things boiled should have the water trapped by a lid, lest the steam take water-soluble vitamins to the heavens with it.

It should also be mentioned that most of the B complex *can* be made in the body—not by the body, but by any of the trillions of crazy bacteria that populate our intestines. These fellows vary in number and variety with a dozen known but unpredictable factors and probably a dozen more one would never have guessed. So, while intestinal flora can sometimes supply some B vitamins to some people, the idea remains useless until science determines when, what, and who.

Another interesting source of the B complex is the drug store. B supplements tend to have one conspicuous but rapidly improving disadvantage—their proportions. These days it's much cheaper for industry to make vitamins from scratch than to torture them out of the biological machines that make them for themselves, but some vitamins cost a lot more than others to synthesize. It costs, for instance, over ten times more to make B_6 than it does to make B_1.

Yeast and wheat, being unconversant with the ins and outs of industrial economics, only make and store vitamins in the proportions they need most; and they happen to do a better job than other plants. For our purposes liver, being geared towards animals, is even better.

Factories, on the other hand, have their foot in the gap between price and cost and are forever trying to widen it. This makes for a tendency to favor the cheapest vitamins when making their multi-vitamin blends. So these days you're liable to find almost anything on the supplement shelf. Some supplements are only as balanced as the last items on the ingredients' list, usually either liver or yeast. Others lack even this saving grace. But still others provide all the possibly important constituents of the complex now known, and in roughly the same proportions found in nature.

The line-up to look for is the one found in the table at the end of the chapter. This represents a rough average of the ratios found in raw living things and wide discrepancies keep us from being too fussy about some of the numbers, especially the ones toward the bottom of the list. But some important ones are often nudged out for no other reason than economy; B_5, B_6 and folic acid in particular. Don't let them get away with it.

Despite all that the B vitamins have in common, each really does have a unique personality of its own—which makes the differences just as interesting.

Nature's B-Complex

For every 1 unit of thiamin, you should expect:
1 unit of riboflavin
10 units of niacin
10 units of pantothenic acid
1 unit of pyridoxine
1/1000 unit of cobalamin
1 unit of folic acid
20 units of para-aminobenzoic acid
500 units of choline
500 units of inositol

Thiamin

Every second of every day of every century, deep in the tumultuous chaos at the center of the sun, atomic nuclei are being smashed into one another to make larger ones. The violence of this process makes the wounded atoms scream their pain in the form of high-energy radiation that streams outward to the planets.

The earth gets in the way of only about a billionth of this energy give-away, but it amounts to something. If you could find an efficient way to convert it, the energy you gather during a minute in the sunshine could zip you around the block in less than a second. Plants spread their green solar cells every spring to collect energy for converting water and carbon dioxide to sugar and oxygen. Our body's job is to reverse this and cash in the precious solar energy without letting the elusive stuff slip away.

We eat the sugar and breathe in the oxygen, give off carbon dioxide and water, and sure enough we can lift our hundred-and-fifty pounds out of bed in the morning with nary a strain. Set a match to wood (which is mostly carbohydrate) and the same thing happens—oxygen gets gobbled up while carbon dioxide, water and energy (a fire) escape. To keep from catching fire, we burn our sugar at 98.6°F using enzymes instead of a match.

Other sugars, be they fruit sugar (fructose), bread sugar (dextrose), milk sugar (lactose), table sugar (sucrose) or malt sugar (maltose), are first converted to glucose before burning. This saves us from having to build separate machinery for each sugar. Glucose, the sugar found in grapes, honey and corn syrup, is a hexagon of carbon atoms with a little hydrogen and oxygen thrown in. Just lopping the hexagon in half gives you back about seven per cent of the energy the sun put in it.

But everybody knows that. Even the lowest bacteria get their energy that way. The real test is what you do with those two three-carbon halves. Yeasts knock a carbon off each, which becomes the carbon dioxide that makes bread rise. The two-carbons that are left become alcohol, which makes people fall.

The whole process is called fermentation and it grinds out enough energy for survival, if you don't mind being a yeast. To make any real progress though, you have to convert those three-carbons into special two-carbons called acetate, the stuff that makes vinegar vinegar. And it's in this ever-so-crucial step that thiamin comes in.

Thiamin happens to have a structure that is perfectly suited for grabbing three-carbons in such a way that a carbon can be easily snapped off. Acetate made in this way is passed along a chain of enzymes that slowly extracts another forty or so per cent of glucose's solar energy.

The enzyme that makes acetate has to have thiamin to do the grabbing because there's nothing else that can, and so must the half-dozen other enzymes that do similar jobs.

These enzymes, and the assembly lines into which they fit, perform their tasks many times a second, making for a lot of wear and tear on the moving parts. Sooner or later the parts are going to wear out, a single day costing thiamin molecules on the order of trillions. The replacements can come from only one source—your food.

If no replacements are forthcoming then acetate is lost as a fuel source, forcing the body to turn to fat-oxidation to satisfy its ravenous energy appetite. But since acetate is also the end-product of fat oxidation, even this gets done inefficiently. Meanwhile toxic three-carbons are accumulating, spilling over into other compartments and clogging up cellular machinery wherever they go. The body can limp along like this for only so long before the symptoms of beriberi set in, meaning severe fatigue and uncoordinated movements as the muscles slowly degenerate into shriveled bands. Even in the early stages the victims are subject to unpredictable heart lapses which can bring about a painful death in a few hours.

As if this weren't enough, a numbness often appears that can lead to complete paralysis. This presents something of a puzzle because nerves, unlike muscles, aren't so acetate-dependent. So it seems that nerve cells have found another use for vitamin B_1, at least when it has three phosphates attached to it.

In the body, phosphates are found all over the place, attached to all kinds of molecules. They act like anti-passports: membranes won't pass a molecule that's attached to one. This way, the cell can keep the things it needs from wandering around and if it decides it does want to move them, it just removes the phosphate with an enzyme called phosphatase. In the case of thiamin the phosphates are added one at a time, diphosphate being the co-enzyme form (the train doesn't stop at monophosphate) and triphosphate being involved in nerve communication.

Nerve fibers criss-cross the body like telephone lines, carrying news to its information clearing-house in the brain, and carrying instructions in the other direction to even the remotest of bodily parts. For all the complexity of the nervous system's tasks, nerve cells themselves can really only do one thing—turn on. If a neuron isn't off it's on, and there's only one on.

The outer membrane of the long fibrous nerve cells separates two groups of ions that are attracted by one of nature's strongest forces—the electromagnetic one. When a signal reaches one end of the fiber, that part of the membrane is instantly depolarized and for one brief moment the two groups rush together, only to be separated again as the membrane repairs itself. This de- and re-polarization zips down the whole fiber till it hits the end, and then it zaps the next cell the same way.

Thiamin triphosphate holds three negatively charged phosphates tightly against the inside of the membrane. There they maintain electric tension with the positively charged ions on the outside. Without thiamin to protect them a phosphatase would slowly pry the phosphates loose and depolarize the membrane—causing over-stimulation. The result would first be tremors and psychosis, then numbness and paralysis as the exhausted nerves finally threw in the towel.

But what's another kick in the pants when you're already on your last leg? The point is that thiamin is necessary and damage can start after even one day without it. One really has to go out of one's way though, not to get it.

All the carbohydrates (starches and the sugars they're built from) that find their way to our dinner table come from plants, plants that use them for energy just like we do. So whenever you find starch in nature you also find thiamin (that's *thi*o, Greek for sulfur which B_1 contains, and vit*amin*). It's usually found very near the surface of such things as peaches, plums, pecans, raspberries, and rice. That's why the novel idea of polishing the coat off of rice brought down millions of Asians with a novel beriberi epidemic. Since facts like these are by now well known, the major source of American carbohydrate, "raped" wheat, is fortified with the vitamin to the extent that eating 24 slices of it will supply the RDA.

But in the two next most important carbohydrates, sugar and alcohol, man in his infinite wisdom has made an oversight no self-respecting vegetable would be guilty of—he left out the thiamin, which is abundant in both sugar cane and the alcohol-making yeast. Sugar-lovers can still get the thiamin they need in the other food they eat, but alcoholics often have no other food. As if this weren't enough, alcohol also blocks intestinal absorption of B vitamins; perhaps having all that alcohol around makes the cells involved afraid to absorb anything.

But heavy drinkers spring a lot of big leaks, and it's only as the ship sinks that thiamin deficiency becomes significant—coming in the form of the horrid hallucinations of delirium tremens, the DTs. But alcoholics rarely die of beriberi, they don't live long enough. Alcoholics, then, may benefit from extra thiamin, as might anyone on a very high-carbohydrate diet. But such supplementation should come in the form of a uniform increase in the whole B complex and its associated minerals.

Thiamin, for instance, very much needs magnesium and manganese in all its functions. Large amounts of B_1 would thus be useless without a parallel increase in those minerals.

In fact, the close contact of these nutrients in the body means that an excreted excess of one would cause excessive excretion of the others, whether they're excess or not. This makes it easier to understand why large thiamin doses can cause manganese deficiency and why the symptoms of thiamin deficiency so closely resemble those of manganese poisoning.

Mild thiamin deficiency often gets blamed for painful tendon cramps, though there are dozens of possible causes. Such pains are especially annoying in the chest area, where they can mimic cardiac distress. Doses given against these and other nerve disorders get as high as six grams a day, or double the *annual* RDA. The thought of what something like that could do to the body's delicately balanced machinery is frightening. Some of those taking such doses have reported experiencing great elation and energy within a few hours, an indication that there really was a thiamin deficiency.

But deficiencies in one B vitamin, mild or otherwise, rarely come alone because B vitamins rarely come alone. So not getting one usually means not getting others as well. This makes the present strategy of tackling each of the forty or more nutrient deficiencies as they come up (and they will come up), instead of correcting the diet problem that generates them, seem like slow torture.

A normal amount of real food cannot help but contain the thiamin RDA and with any care at all (pork, nuts, beans and grains) will have it several times over. Any individual who really needs more has a serious (and probably genetic) problem and should be seeing a doctor, not a vitamin salesman. But even if you eat as much as you need, it's not impossible to get a thiamin deficiency.

Since there is not and has never been a cell that can survive without thiamin, it's a real surprise to find life forms that go out of their way to destroy it. Whatever their reason for doing so, it's nothing for us to worry about unless we happen to eat them—because the enzyme that does it for them will do it for us too, if it finds its way into our stomachs. The enzyme is called thiaminase and is made by clams especially, though also by other sea-dwelling delicacies. But if they're cooked they're safe, because thiaminase is destroyed by heat.

But how do you cook the bacteria in your stomach? In Japan whole towns have been afflicted by something called "thiaminase disease", caused by a bacterium that makes an enzyme that destroys all the thiamin these poor people eat. These bacteria can be transmitted from person to person (yes, via excrement) and the unlucky recipients come down with what might just as well be beriberi. For the moment though, this disease shows little interest in Americans. But Americans have problems of their own.

Thiamin, as it happens, decomposes very quickly and very permanently in an alkaline environment, a fact that holds for other B vitamins as well. Though food usually inclines toward acidity anyway, the stomach secretes a generous amount of hydrochloric acid just to make sure, and it has other important reasons for doing so as well.

And then we have products like milk of magnesia (magnesium hydroxide), sodium bicarbonate and all the seltzers and antacids that grace our medicine cabinets, all of which are especially designed to set up an alkaline (the alka in Alka-Seltzer) environment in the stomach, leaving it effectively bound and gagged for hours. Next time, before you swallow something that promises to absorb forty-seven times its weight of your precious stomach acid, think.

Nowadays the preferred form of synthetic thiamin is

thiamin hydrochloride, which has its own molecule of hydrochloric acid built in.

Seen against the whole spectrum of B vitamins, thiamin in many ways stands out from the rest. It is, for instance, the B least bound to its respective enzymes, and is therefore the one with the shortest storage time. It's also the one most sensitive to heat. Actually it tolerates heat reasonably well, but the pulverizing, grinding, sterilizing and pressure cooking used in food processing often involve much higher temperatures than a thiamin molecule would normally run into.

Thiamin's also interesting in that how much of it you should eat depends on what else you're eating. Basically, someone consuming 2000 calories should also consume a milligram of B_1, provided his diet has a normal proportion (about 40%) of carbohydrates. More food, especially more carbohydrates, means more thiamin.

But if man was meant to rely on vitamin books to stay healthy, he'd have been born with one in his hip pocket. As it is, such things are taken care of for us: more foods in their natural forms (especially carbohydrates) *have* more thiamin.

Thiamin (mg/100 gm)

The vitamin concentrations are expressed in milligrams (thousandths of a gram) per 100 grams of food, or thousandths of a gram per hundred. To convert them to percents (what percentage of the food is thiamin), divide by a thousand. For parts per million, multiply by ten.

whisky, wine, tea,		oysters	0.14
corn syrup, coffee,		mackerel	0.15
honey and soda	0.00	lamb	0.15
human milk	0.01	eggs	0.17
soy lecithin	0.01	sprouts	0.18
goat's milk	0.01	salmon	0.21
eggwhite	0.01	barley	0.21
cow milk	0.03	almonds	0.24
cheeses	0.03	liver	0.25
fruits	0.03	blackstrap molasses	0.28
radishes	0.03	chickpeas	0.31
shrimp	0.03	egg yolk	0.32
sardines	0.03	walnuts	0.33
skim milk	0.04	rice	0.34
yogurt	0.04	corn	0.37
onions	0.04	lentils	0.37
cucumbers	0.04	mature sprouts	0.40
tuna	0.05	rye	0.43
coconut	0.05	hazelnuts	0.46
Barbados molasses	0.06	eel	0.50
chicken	0.06	wheat	0.57
light molasses	0.07	oats	0.60
oranges	0.07	buckwheat	0.60
vegetables	0.08	beans	0.68
cow meat	0.08	pig meat	0.70
medium molasses	0.09	millet	0.73
pineapple	0.09	peas	0.80
mushrooms	0.10	alfalfa	0.80
clams	0.10	pecans	0.86
avocado	0.11	bee pollen	0.93
turkey	0.11	brazil nuts	0.96
potatoes	0.11	sesame seeds	0.98
veal	0.13	soybeans	1.10

peanuts	1.2	sunflower seeds	2.2
piñon nuts	1.3	torula yeast	15.
royal jelly	1.5	brewer's yeast	16.
wheat germ	2.0		

Recommended Daily Allowances
for Thiamin

	men	women
birth - 3 years	0.7 mg	
3 - 6 years	0.9	
7 - 10 years	1.2	
11 - 14 years	1.4	1.1
15 - 22 years	1.5	1.2
23+	1.2	1.0
pregnant women		1.5
lactating women		1.5

Riboflavin

For better or for worse, things never stop changing in this world. What was useful yesterday is obsolete today, what was brand new is now discarded. And so it is in the detailed workings of life, where molecules are constantly torn apart, overhauled, rebuilt and finally sent to the junkyard by the body's machine shop.

To make a molecule, you need parts. The parts are also made of parts; the atoms of life being hydrogen (H), carbon (C), oxygen (O), nitrogen (N), sulfur (S) and phosphorus (P).

For your molecular recipe you might need an amide (NH), an amino (NHH) or an ammonia (NHHH) group. You might choose carboxyl (CO), hydroxyl (OH) or sulfhydryl (SH) components. For spice you may want methyls (CHHH), phosphates (POOO), aldehydes (COH) or ketos (CO) in your formula. To complete your molecule, just attach the selected accessories to a hydrocarbon (CH) chain of whatever length. That can be straight, crooked or circular, your choice. Whatever you come up with, odds are that some ancient microbe has already tried it.

The molecules of life have plenty of carbon, oxygen and nitrogen, but there's nothing they have plenty of like hydrogen. Hydrogen is not only the atom most plentiful in life, it's also the one most abundant in the universe at large. It's also the simplest, composed of only a single positively-charged proton and a single negatively-charged electron.

So, on any of the many occasions when the body has to take a molecule apart—either to release energy in the process or because the molecule is dangerous in its present form—it's quite possible a hydrogen atom will have to be chipped off at some point in the process. And any worker who's skilled at that particular specialty is sure to find a secure position with the body.

Riboflavin got the job. Riboflavin happens to have this nitrogen atom that is just about the loneliest atom in the world. It has two negatively charged electrons that have to share the favors of a single carbon nucleus of the opposite electromagnetic sex. Now what that nitrogen atom would like more than anything in the world is to find a nice hydrogen atom for one of these electrons so that each could have a nucleus of its own. And riboflavin has not one but two such nitrogens.

So along comes an enzyme that's specially designed to grip a molecule that has one hydrogen too many. All it has to do now is bind one of these riboflavins to itself, hold the molecule in just the right position, and riboflavin will pluck off the two desired hydrogen atoms, one with each of its two under-satisfied nitrogens. In this way vitamin B_2 plays a key role in neutralizing the agents of damage that are forever finding their way into our bodies: take two hydrogens off a poison like nicotine and, being no longer nicotine, it's no longer a poison.

The same process, de-hydrogen-ation, is the first in a series of energy-liberating transfers that make up the means by which, more than any other single thing, animal life was able to develop and flourish in this world. Like bullets ricocheting in a steel chamber, the separated proton and electron of each energy-charged hydrogen atom cascade down a pair of parallel energy-absorbing ladders until their energy is spent. The exhausted particles are then rejoined and picked up by an oxygen atom to make HOH, water.

In all, riboflavin is known to be necessary to over a dozen enzymes that do this sort of thing. Sometimes they like their co-enzyme in the form of riboflavin phosphate (alias FMN, for "flavin mononucleotide") though most prefer it combined with two phosphates and the amino acid-like adenine to make FAD, flavin adenine dinucleotide. Food riboflavin is also found in both these forms, animal products predominating in them and plants more often having the free form. Which way the vitamin comes to you is of little real importance though, as long as the body has enough magnesium to properly move the phosphates around.

Once FMN or FAD finds the enzyme that's looking for it, the pair can be very hard to separate. This exceptionally tight binding makes riboflavin the co-enzyme that sticks with the body longest in times of trouble.

Vitamin B_2 is also one of the lucky three vitamins that's put back into some of the grain products it's removed from. Not only that but they put back *more* than they take out, thanks to an early over-estimate of wheat's riboflavin content.

Riboflavin is also the vitamin most resistant to the ravages of heat, an enemy that threatens death by disintegration to most all of the chemicals of life. But cooking temperatures of a 100°C or less have little effect on riboflavin. What's interesting about this is that neither water nor the things it contains ever get much hotter than 100°C, the temperature at which water boils, regardless of how hot the stove gets. This means that food cooked in water has about as many riboflavins when it comes out as it had when it went in, excepting those that went for a dip in the cooking water (so don't throw it out).

The same promise can't be made for things fried in oil, because oils have boiling points nearly double that of water. A temperature like this asks too much of delicate organic molecules.

It's riboflavin's excellent heat-resistance which, with its storage properties, makes it a difficult vitamin not to get. Or at least it tries, but it labors always under an inborn handicap because it's extremely vulnerable to light.

Light is moving energy, traveling in containers. You can tell how much energy the container contains by the color of the light. As you range the rainbow from red to blue, the colors you pass become increasingly energetic. One of these colors, a slightly purplish blue, is composed of containers (also called photons or quanta) whose energy is just what riboflavin has a weakness for. When such a photon strikes a molecule of vitamin B_2 it gets absorbed, and the absorbed energy is enough to shake riboflavin into another structure, one for which the body has no use.

But it's possible that even this seeming liability has been put to good use by the ever-adaptable human body; giving riboflavin a secondary function as a photon scavenger. If this is true it means that vitamin B_2 would stand between the ravaging effects of light (though there are of course some good ones too) and the delicate light-sensitive molecules of cells that are exposed to it. Especially vulnerable are the cells that live just inside our essentially transparent skin, and those that occasionally travel to that territory via the blood and lymph systems.

The skin cells themselves are basically dead ones so they

don't need protection, but there is one part of the body that is in constant contact with light and is very much alive. And the eye does in fact suffer damage during riboflavin deficiency, nearly every kind of eye problem having been blamed on it. At one time or another the problems have included itching, burning, blinking, excessive pupil dilation, eyestrain, focusing difficulty, pinkeye and distortions of the visual field.

Riboflavin deficiency may actually cause all those things, but having them doesn't necessarily mean having riboflavin deficiency at all. The fact is that nobody is really too sure what a riboflavin deficiency is. To find out you have to do two things. First you have to somehow prepare meals without one iota of riboflavin in them, and that's not easy. Next you have to find someone who's going to eat those meals while you watch him fall apart. That's not easy either.

If you do get that far about the worst you can expect to see in your volunteer is a lot of sore throats. Try it on an animal though, and it might drop dead in a month.

Without trying to make sense out of all this, it looks like the ordinary American needn't worry too much about this vitamin. And about the best advice one can give is not to sign up for any riboflavin deficiency experiments. People whose bodies get a lot of light (sunbathers, sex film stars, etc.) might need a little extra. So might people who take a lot of poison.

Riboflavin is as sensitive to alkali as thiamin is, so sodium bicarbonate should be restricted to external use only. And finally, light strips away all of riboflavin's heat-resistance, another reason to cover your food as it cooks.

Next vitamin. . . .

Riboflavin (mg/100 gms)

gelatin, oils	0.00	clams	0.18
wine	0.01	sprouts	0.19
fruits	0.02	corn	0.19
watercress	0.02	raw milk	0.19
coconut	0.02	cow meat	0.20
shrimp	0.03	broccoli	0.20
celery	0.03	pig meat	0.20
beer	0.03	Barbados molasses	0.20
soy lecithin	0.03	turkey	0.20
honey	0.04	spinach	0.20
tomatoes	0.04	beans	0.22
mayonnaise	0.04	rye	0.22
onions	0.04	lentils	0.22
papaya	0.04	eggwhite	0.22
peaches	0.04	sesame seeds	0.24
cabbage	0.04	cottage cheese	0.25
rice	0.05	parsley	0.25
carrots	0.05	blackstrap molasses	0.25
herring	0.05	peas	0.25
lettuce	0.05	lamb	0.27
light molasses	0.06	sunflower seeds	0.28
strawberries	0.07	eggs	0.28
barley	0.07	veal	0.31
raspberries	0.09	soybeans	0.31
goat's milk	0.11	mushrooms	0.33
brazil nuts	0.12	chicken	0.36
medium molasses	0.12	millet	0.38
vegetables	0.12	human milk	0.40
fishes	0.12	cheeses	0.46
wheat	0.12	egg yolk	0.52
peanuts	0.13	mustard greens	0.64
walnuts	0.13	wheat germ	0.68
pecans	0.13	almonds	0.92
oats	0.14	bee pollen	1.7
cream cheese	0.15	alfalfa	1.8
chickpeas	0.15	royal jelly	1.9
buckwheat	0.17	liver	4.1
cow milk	0.17	brewer's yeast	4.2
yogurt	0.18	torula yeast	16.

Recommended Daily Allowances
for Riboflavin

	men		women
birth - 3 years		0.8 mg	
4 - 6 years		1.1	
7 - 10 years		1.2	
11 - 14 years	1.5		1.3
15 - 22 years	1.8		1.4
23 - 50 years	1.6		1.2
51+	1.3		1.1
pregnant women			1.7
lactating women			1.9

Niacin

Niacin does the same thing as riboflavin. Just like B_2, B_3 can reach into a molecule and come out with two of that molecule's hydrogens. But niacin is necessary because there are hydrogens and there are hydrogens. Some detach easily enough for riboflavin to do the job, but for the really tough cookies you need niacin. And it turns out that the great majority of hydrogens fall into the second category.

Niacin, when attached to an appropriate enzyme, can wrench off even the most firmly stuck hydrogens, and hold those hydrogens loosely enough for riboflavin to remove them and start them on their way down the electron transport chain. In the course of being passed from B_3 to B_2 the energy of the electron drops considerably. But that energy isn't just scattered to the wayward winds, it's carefully harnessed to recharge the body's energy battery, ATP.

An adenosine tri-phosphate molecule is like a loaded gun. It can be put on the shelf until necessity calls. When the time comes, a special enzyme will come along and pull the trigger, firing a sizzling phosphate bullet out to do the work at hand. Adenosine *tri*-phosphate is now adenosine *di*-phosphate, a gun which the energy derived from the sun (via food) is channelled toward reloading for another occasion.

Without niacin, the 200 or more enzymes that require it for their activities begin to close up shop. This means that de-hydrogen-ation reactions, whether for energy gathering, poison detoxification or making compounds essential to the body's operation, come to a virtual standstill that riboflavin isn't strong enough to relieve. The consequences of course are serious: a bout with insanity and intense diarrhea that ends in death. The whole syndrome is called pellagra (Italian for "skin dry", one of the less distressing symptoms), a disease that ravaged the American South for a century. Nobody seemed to pay much attention until another pellagra epidemic was kindled in the European South. Only when concerned Europeans sat up and took notice did anyone get on the trail of the cause, and the cause was corn. This wonder crop didn't even exist in Europe until trans-ocean travel brought Columbus and his thousands of relatives over to the "New World" and brought corn back to the Old. Unlike the Indians, who'd had thousands of years of experience eating corn and knew how to use it wisely, the colonists seized on the hardy new plant as a substitute for other grains. And of course communication with the ignorant Indians was a rarity. The problems didn't really start until the world's poor began turning to corn as a cheap, easy-to-grow substitute for a balanced meal. The more remote regions of the South soon became known for such distinctive delicacies as corn pone and hominy grits, and for its thousands of cases of pellagra.

But, being a disease of the poor, it didn't much interest the doctors of that time. It wasn't till their European colleagues kicked up some comment that they found the what if not the why behind pellagra.

An analysis of corn and its products reveals that they all contain plenty of niacin. So it seems that something else in the corn was either preventing the absorption of niacin or was out and out destroying the vitamin. Actually though, even if they never saw a niacin molecule, the pellagra-sufferers need not have been pellagra-sufferers. It turns out that a little more quantity and variety of protein in their diets could have completely prevented the disease.

Of the 22 amino acids that go into (and can be taken out of) elaborate protein molecules, there is one that looks a lot like niacin. And it happens that the body has found a way to convert that amino acid, tryptophan, into niacin. But it also happens that tryptophan is one of those eight amino acids that the body doesn't know how to make. That means you have to eat more tryptophan if you don't get enough niacin. But tryptophan is found in protein and poor people could as little afford beef for its tryptophan content as for its niacin. And corn finds itself a particularly unreliable tryptophan source.

Put all the pieces together and you have the pellagra picture. Unless one prefers to see it as Geronimo's Revenge, the whole tragedy stands as a monument to the importance of honest communication, not only with our fellow travelers, but with the whole cosmos of life.

When niacin is eaten, the body first attaches an amide group to it. We now have niacinamide. To the niacinamide are added phosphates and adenine to make niacinamide adenine dinucleotide, or NAD for short. Another phosphate makes NAD into NAD phosphate, or NADP.

NAD, with or without the P, is the form of the vitamin

that actually goes in there and works with the enzymes, in fact the enzymes won't work without it. When a given niacin molecule has outlived its usefulness, it's shipped to the liver. The liver sticks a methyl group on it and sends it on its way out of the body via the kidney.

So what? The body's lost a methyl group. What's a methyl group anyhow?

All the body's cells are forever prepared for emergencies. Mostly they go on doing their work as best they can, and the job they do is terrific. But there often comes a time when the body must, little though it likes to, ask for more. On these special occasions the cell machinery works overtime, calling enzymes back from vacations and diverting workers from less important tasks to concentrate on whatever it happens to be that that cell can help the body with during an emergency. The cells are always anxious to cooperate and will at least attempt whatever is asked of them. In this way the body is able to shift into third whenever the need arises and return to normal when the storm blows over. The catch is that the change-over has got to be temporary, because the cell often suspends vital operations on the understanding that it can shortly return to them when the crisis has passed.

And then, just like when your car is run at a hundred miles an hour, parts wear out much more quickly and fuel is burned very inefficiently. In fact, when things finally calm down for the cell, it's likely to need a shorter workweek or even a rest before resuming its everyday chores. Needless to say, anything that's able to make this overhaul in the body's functions is a very powerful thing indeed. It can alter nearly every aspect of a person's life, being capable of life-saving changes when used correctly, and damage or death when not.

Dotting the outside surface of every cell are tiny receptors, little specially shaped niches that are most of the time empty, waiting for the perfectly-shaped key to come along and fit itself inside them. When it does, the lock turns and a chain of events begins that eventually brings on the crisis response in that particular cell, with different types of cells responding in different ways. That special key, the one that ignites the whole process, is called a hormone.

Every kind of hormone has a different shape, and whether a cell is going to respond to a given hormone depends on whether that cell was born with receptors that have a shape into which that particular hormone fits. One of the more innocuous hormones is something called noradrenalin.

Noradrenalin causes blood vessels to constrict and in the brain has the special function of relaying messages across the gap between two nerve cells. And there's something similar to noradrenalin called adrenalin.

Although it's chemically similar to noradrenalin, adrenalin is a different story altogether. Adrenalin actually does the same general things as noradrenalin, but it does them about six times stronger. And, although adrenalin also constricts blood vessels in many parts of the body, it compensates by opening others up, namely those of the brain and muscles. So, while other parts of the body are getting less blood, our thinking and acting apparati are literally swimming in fuel. Not only is there more blood, but the blood is especially rich in glucose, the fuel that the brain and muscles most like.

The overall effect is a panic response. Ideas flood and race through the mind while the body follows compulsively, feeling like there's no time for conscious thought. In such a state anything seems possible and many normally impossible things suddenly aren't. It's basically a case of temporary hysteria, usually triggered by desperation.

The effects of adrenalin and noradrenalin are so different that it's hard to believe that it all boils down to one tiny methyl group: Adrenalin is made by attaching a methyl to noradrenalin. And then there's DMT.

DMT has a well-deserved reputation for being the most potent (if shortest acting) of the hallucinogens circulating on America's big black market for drugs. Like all the psychedelic substances, DMT brings about a radical change in the user's relationship with reality, by altering the only handle by which he can grip reality—his senses. So much for a chemical that certainly doesn't belong in the brain. Serotonin is one that does.

The brain makes serotonin by adding an amino group to an amino acid. This mades tryptophan into tryptamine. Now just add a hydroxyl group to tryptamine and you have serotonin. If, instead of a hydroxyl, you add two methyls you get di-methyl tryptamine, DMT.

We know that serotonin helps make us fall into deep sleeps but we also know it does a lot more, though just what else it does is still anyone's guess. Meanwhile one can't help but notice that practically all the famous hallucinogenic drugs look an awful lot like serotonin. See for yourself.

First, notice that LSD, psilocybin (from the Mexican magic mushroom), bufotenine (from *amanita muscaria*, the Siberian magic mushroom), and DMT all would be mistaken for serotonin if seen from the underside. Second, look at all those methyl groups! If it weren't for two methyls, bufotenine would be serotonin and DMT would practically be tryptamine. The more you look at it the more it looks like it's the methyls that put the trip in tryptamine. Without it's methyls LSD would be LSA, the relatively non-

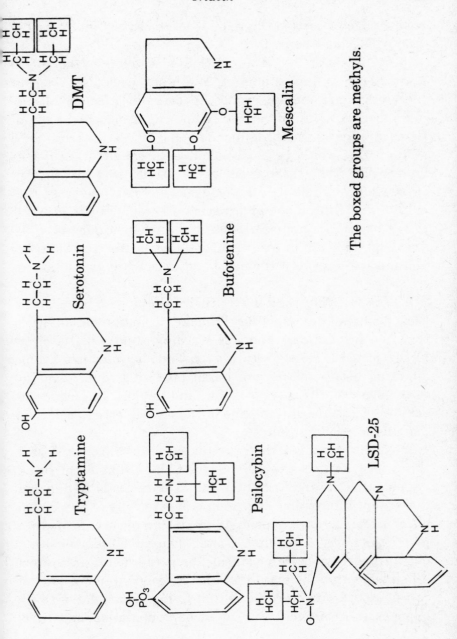

The boxed groups are methyls.

hallucinogenic active ingredient of morning glory seeds. And what about mescalin?

Mescalin doesn't look as much like serotonin (though it also resembles amphetamine). The best psychedelic credentials it has are methyl groups all over the place. Add one more methyl to it and you get something about one hundred times stronger, something nicknamed STP.

All of this would be as academic as it sounds were it not for the fact that there seem to be people who are in the psychedelic state on an all-day, every day basis; without the help of any flipped-out pharmacist. Throughout history, society's psychotics and schizophrenics have been viewed with a strange mixture of awe and contempt; revered as mystics and medicine men on the one hand, burned at the stake on the other.

It's the fact that they live in their own private little world that inspires contempt, for it makes communication with these people difficult and unrewarding. And when society feels rejected it rejects accordingly. This, perhaps more than anything else, explains the harsh laws this country maintains against the psychedelics, and makes the right to achieve this state of mind one of the civil liberties society is most reluctant to grant.

What distinguishes the drug-taking schizos from the real thing is willingness to believe the things that seem to be happening but aren't. While the tripper finds a dancing flower an interesting but temporary novelty, the schizophrenic feels himself hopelessly trapped in a world he doesn't understand. As a result he often panics, either rebelling outward with violence or suicide; or withdrawing in toward a helpless catatonic state in which he might remain for the rest of his life, if you can call that living. This kind of thing happens to about one percent of our population and that, whether measured in countless lives rendered useless or in lost man-hours, adds up to a lot of misfortune. So if someone says he has a way to spare us this misfortune he deserves a listen, even if he says he's doing it with half a pound of vitamin XYZ administered through the navel every third minute.

What's really being suggested is niacin, given in doses of from one to thirty grams a day. But to see the reaction of orthodox medicine to the idea, you'd think it was half a pound of XYZ . . . etc. A gram isn't anything to be afraid of though. If you dipped a damp fingertip into flour, a gram is about what you'd remove.

Meanwhile niacin has turned thousands of mental patients into former mental patients, often cutting through a lifetime of confusion in a few weeks. It doesn't matter for these people that nobody's sure *how* niacin works (maybe all that stuff about methyl groups is just a cute coincidence). If we should stop doing everything we don't completely understand then we should as well stop living, one of the things we understand least. It's worth mentioning though that niacin won't work its wonders for everyone. Whether it'll work for you seems to depend on your histamine.

One of the reasons toilets flush is so you don't have to look at your urine. But doctors don't feel that way at all; they love to look at your urine. They've found that by studying it carefully they can find out a lot of things about you that even your best friends don't know. (If you find this surprising, try looking through your neighbor's garbage can some time. You can learn a lot.) Some schizophrenics have a lot of histamine in their urine. Well we know that if they have enough to throw away they certainly have enough, so they can take care of themselves. Other schizophrenics excrete abnormally low amounts of histamine. Maybe we can do something for them.

Histamine, by the way, is a chemical the body makes from the amino acid histidine (the same way it makes tryptamine from tryptophan) and stores in special cells for the proper occasion. When these cells decide to release it into the bloodstream, histamine travels to the tiny blood vessels under the skin and makes their walls flimsier. As a result, water leaks out of the blood plasma and starts to accumulate in the nearby tissue. The extra water is what makes the area around bruises swell a little. It also swells nasal passages during allergy or disease, an effect that antihistamines try to counteract. In the stomach, histamine increases secretions of enzymes and hydrochloric acid, and in the brain. . . . well, we're not sure yet, but it seems to slow things down a little, make people more peaceful.

Besides allergies, colds and brass knuckles, one thing that really makes those histamine-releasing cells want to release their histamine is niacin. Within minutes of taking any sizeable niacin dose the histamine reaction can be felt, coming in the form of a burning flush through the upper part of the body that lasts an uncomfortable hour.

Histamine released in this way won't do anything for the brain though, otherwise why bother giving niacin to schizophrenics when we could just shoot them up with histamine? The problem is that the brain bars the door to histamine from any other part of the body. The door is in a wall called the blood-brain barrier, a membrane that covers most of the brain. The guard at the door is very careful about what's allowed to enter the brain's sensitive tissues, and histamine is not on the welcome list. So any histamine that's going to be in the brain has to be made and released right on the premises.

Whether niacin can promote this kind of thing in the brain or not is still uncertain, but there are many reports of niacin increasing the effect of tranquilizers to such an extent that they can be withdrawn altogether. There are also claims that niacin acts as an antidote to drugs of the psychedelic family.

What it all adds up to is still unclear, because the pieces we have now are only enough to tell us that the puzzle is interesting; we can't claim a solution. The low-histamine schizophrenics make up about a third of those who have the disease. Medicine hopes to be able to help this third with nutrition. Let's keep our fingers crossed.

Having your methyl groups flushed out or your histamine raised is all very well if you've too many methyls or too little histamine, as schizophrenics seem to have. If you're normal to begin with you won't be normal any more after you've taken a lot of niacin. Remember that the liver has to attach a methyl group to each and every molecule of niacin that you ingest. And a gram of niacin has fifty billion trillion such molecules. That's rather a lot (!) of work to ask of your already hard-working liver unless there's a special reason for it. This also means fifty quintillion methyl groups shot to hell when your body might have had other plans for them. Maybe that's why people taking several grams a day so often suffer liver damage. But even if it isn't, people who already have a liver problem should consider whether they need another one.

The stepped-up stomach secretions induced by histamine that's induced by niacin could spell trouble for people with ulcers. And then, niacin is also an acid, something ulcer sufferers don't need a few extra grams of in their stomachs. The amide form of vitamin B_3 could be considered, being neither an acid nor a pro-histamine. But then again niacinamide is more likely to cause liver problems. You can't win.

Warnings notwithstanding, niacin is often recommended in large quantities to improve circulation in the elderly, which it can do via its effects on histamine. It's also used to lower blood cholesterol. Niacin's ability to do this may have something to do with its acidity. But if it will make the blood acidic it can do the same for the urine, and acidic urine invites gout. One also hears of niacin worsening the effects of diabetes, and even causing it.

So much for the problem of getting too much; though, getting what your body needs for optimum operation shouldn't be hard. Niacin is easily the most abundant co-enzyme, is the cheapest B vitamin to make and, like thiamin and riboflavin, is replaced in many de-vitaminized grain products. Both niacin and its amide are available in supplement form, the amide being a little cheaper. The idea of combining niacin and riboflavin is for the benefit of riboflavin, which has a hard time dissolving in water. This could be useful if you don't like pills and prefer taking it in, rather than with, a glass of water.

You may, in your vitamin shopping, run across something called nicotinic acid. This is niacin traveling under an alias. This extra name has the advantage of allowing us to confuse it with nicotine, the addictive nerve stimulant found in tobacco. The structures of niacin and nicotine are somewhat alike, but the body is unable to take advantage of the similarity and convert the poison into a vitamin. It may be only a coincidence but niacin has been reported to make kicking the nicotine habit a little easier. Of course niacinamide should have an alias too, it's nicotinamide.

Niacin (mg/100 gm)

sugar	0.00	brazil nuts	1.6
mayonnaise	0.01	cashews	1.8
soy lecithin	0.01	chickpeas	2.0
cream	0.04	lentils	2.0
apples	0.07	blackstrap molasses	2.1
chard	0.07	corn	2.2
watermelon	0.08	soybeans	2.2
grapefruit	0.08	millet	2.3
yogurt	0.08	beans	2.4
milk	0.08	oysters	2.5
pecans	0.09	mature sprouts	2.6
tangerines	0.09	peas	2.6
cheeses	0.10	shrimp	3.3
eggwhite	0.10	almonds	3.5
wine	0.10	barley	3.7
plums	0.19	wheat germ	4.2
cucumbers	0.20	mushrooms	4.2
eggs	0.20	wheat	4.3
grapes	0.20	buckwheat	4.3
human milk	0.20	piñon nuts	4.5
light molasses	0.20	wheat bran	4.7
celery	0.25	rice	4.7
radishes	0.25	potatoes	4.8
coffee	0.26	alfalfa	5.0
cabbage	0.28	cow meat	5.0
goat's milk	0.30	sesame seeds	5.4
coconut	0.44	sardines	5.4
honey	0.48	pig meat	5.5
fruits	0.60	sunflower seeds	5.6
beer	0.61	veal	7.8
vegetables	0.65	royal jelly	8.2
walnuts	0.71	halibut	9.2
sprouts	0.80	rabbit	11.
peaches	0.87	turkey	11.
raspberries	0.89	swordfish	11.
hazelnuts	0.90	tuna	12
oats	1.00	chicken	12
bleu cheese	1.2	salmon	13
medium molasses	1.2	liver	16
clams	1.3	peanuts	17
collard greens	1.3	bee pollen	19
avocado	1.6	brewer's yeast	38
rye	1.6	torula yeast	100

The Vitamin Book

Recommended Daily Allowances
for Niacin

	men	women
birth - 6 months	5 mg	
6 months - 1 year	8	
1 - 3 years	9	
4 - 6 years	12	
7 - 10 years	16	
11 - 14 years	18	16
15 - 22 years	20	14
23 - 50 years	18	13
51+	16	12
pregnant women		18
lactating women		20

Vitamin B$_4$

No one lives at this address.

At one time or another all these B numbers have been vitaminized, but the things they were affixed to turned out to be something other than was originally thought, often mixtures of vitamins that already had numbers, amino acids, or strange substances required by birds or rats but of no importance whatsoever to people.

The only B numbers still in use are 1, 2, 3, 5, 6, 12, 15 and 17, but there is a campaign being waged to recycle all those other numbers. If they had their way this chapter'd have been about choline and other B vitamins would also get spanking new numbers. Biotin would get seven, inositol eight, folic acid nine, and PABA ten.

Other B vitamin candidates needn't worry though, there are still plenty of numbers left.

Pantothenic Acid

Virtually all the energy our bodies use gets locked up, at some point in the process, as acetate. It may start out as protein, fat or carbohydrate but if it's going to finish as energy you can bet acetate is somewhere in the middle. So the process of extracting energy from it is of central importance to the energy-dependent animal kingdom.

Picture a group of lazy enzymes sitting in a circle around a lazy-susan. Then somebody comes along and drops an acetate molecule in front of one of the enzymes. That enzyme takes a bite out of it and wheels what remains over to the enzyme on his left. After he's taken his bite the process continues until it gets back around to the first enzyme, by that time, everyone has had a bite and there's nothing left. So what has pantothenic acid to do with all this? Pantothenic acid is the lazy-susan. Or at least it's part of it. The rest consists of oxalo-acetate, mercapto-ethylamine, adenine and, you guessed it, phosphate. These things the body can make for itself, pantothenic acid it cannot. When these elements are working together they act as a handle by which acetate can be grasped while it's being slowly taken apart.

Originally, acetate is made up of two carbon atoms, two oxygens and four hydrogens. To the carbon and oxygen, the body adds two oxygens of its own (from the air we breathe in) to produce two carbon dioxides (the air we breathe out). But it's the hydrogens that really generate energy. Each has its electron whipped down the electron transport chain with an ATP being "loaded" at each big step along the way.

But acetate isn't always broken down. Sometimes it's built up, about a dozen acetates being necessary to make cholesterol, among other things. The other things are steroids, a class of complex chemicals that the body uses as hormones, cortisone and the sex hormones among them. The cortex of our adrenal glands devotes the bulk of its energies to putting together acetates and turning out steroids. The steroids in turn perform humdrum duties during humdrum times, just waiting for the right opportunity to show what they can really do. Their shining hour is a period of stress.

In emergency situations the outer part of the adrenal glands let go with a burst of adrenalin, then adrenalin goes up to the pituitary gland, chairman of the endocrine board, and persuades it to allow the insides (the cortices; singular: cortex) of the adrenal glands to release adrenal steroids, like cortisone. It's through these that adrenalin is able to work its wonders on the sugar content of the blood. The guys who really deserve the credit are the cortical steroids.

Without them the body is easily worn out by the demands made on it by such things as overwork, disease, poisoning, extremes of hot and cold, injury, allergy, hunger, and emotional distress. The worn-out body then develops new signs—fatigue, constipation, loss of appetite and susceptibility to infection among them—and progresses to outright stress diseases—like arthritis, allergies, and ulcers of the stomach—when the situation becomes chronic.

The natural reaction is to replace the missing steroids in

pill form. But then it's no longer your body that finely tunes the amount you need to the amount you get, but your doctor. Wise as he may be, he's helpless to predict the incessant metabolic adjustments your body makes in the course of a day. So you're either getting too much or too little. What happens when you get too little we know already, it's what the steroids were originally prescribed for, but the other side of the coin isn't much prettier. Too high a steroid level means high blood pressure, wounds that won't heal, fragile bones, steroid addiction, weight gain and personality disturbances.

And what about the poor adrenal cortex? It was just about out of business when all this started and still nothing has been done to reverse whatever caused the problem in the first place. The next time you look in on it there may be nothing left but blood, pus, and scar tissue. This may not seem too important to you if you seem to be getting along fine on your oral cortisone, but that cortex used to make a lot more than just cortisone. You may wind up trying to replace cortisol, deoxycortisol, corticosterone, deoxycortisterone, and aldosterone as well. There must be a better way.

Since all the steroids look like they were made from cholesterol, maybe eating more cholesterol would improve the body's ability to make steroids. There's even the tempting possibility that the current low-cholesterol food fad may be aggravating stress diseases in this country. What little we know about this subject indicates that there is a subtle difference between the way the body handles home-made cholesterol and what it does with the imported stuff. The former seems to have the better chance of eventually becoming steroid, the latter of being deposited inside a blood vessel.

The simple and safe way to dodge both addiction and

atherosclerosis is to supply enough pantothenic acid and then just sit back and watch nature take its course. The industrious enzymes of the adrenal cortex will thus have the ability to grind out steroids so as to exactly fill the body's needs without any danger of exceeding them. But making steroids is only one of cholesterol's functions in the body.

Just as blood needs an airtight vessel to carry it, so does the information transmitted through our nerves need some kind of barrier to keep it all from leaking out before it reaches its destination. A telephone line uses rubber for insulation, our nerves use myelin.

Myelin is a thin, fatty, sheet-like membrane that wraps itself around the nerve fiber like toilet paper around a cardboard tube. Here it serves not only to keep the all-important signal from dissipating, but to protect neighboring cells from the violent electro-chemical activity that's routine for neurons but ravaging to other cells.

The components of myelin are fitted together in just such a way as to hold the whole membrane tightly together. Remove one brick and the whole structure is liable to fall apart, allowing voracious free radicals to squeeze through the door. And as they attack the soft underbelly of the membrane, they convert what used to be membrane into more free radicals. These free radicals gobble up more membrane and then they in turn. . . . well, once you've got this far there's no end in sight.

And cholesterol happens to be one of these myelin components. We also know that acetate and pantothenic acid are needed for the body to make its own cholesterol. So when there are numerous reports of pantothenic acid deficiency giving rise to nerve de-myelin-ation, one can't help but think that it all adds up to something.

Accordingly, vitamin B_5 is now admitted to be "essential

to human nutrition", "essential" meaning you eat it or you die. It doesn't seem to be essential enough though, to discourage its deliberate removal in the refining of grains. So white flour winds up with about half the pantothenate of wheat flour, while Uncle Ben's-type precooked rice has a quarter of what the grain started out with. Avoid foods like these and you avoid the problem.

If a balanced diet won't satisfy your craving for this vitamin, then there are certainly pills that will. They provide it either as pantothenic acid or as calcium pantothenate, the latter having the advantage of added calcium. Of course you pay for that advantage, but it's only money.

Pantothenic Acid (mg/100 gm)

soy lecithin	0.05	perch	0.80
beer	0.10	walnuts	0.90
eggwhite	0.14	turkey	0.90
oysters	0.20	sardines	0.90
fruits	0.20	chicken	0.90
honey	0.20	mushrooms	1.00
coconut	0.20	avocado	1.1
cream	0.20	chickpeas	1.2
brazil nuts	0.23	cashews	1.3
blackberries	0.25	lobster	1.5
blackstrap molasses	0.30	bleu cheese	1.8
vegetables	0.30	wheat germ	2.2
milk	0.30	bee pollen	2.2
shrimp	0.30	eggs	2.3
halibut	0.30	rye	2.6
clams	0.30	peanuts	2.8
bran	0.35	wheat	3.2
beans	0.40	alfalfa	3.3
skim milk	0.40	peas	3.6
almonds	0.50	egg yolk	4.2
cheeses	0.50	lentils	4.8
broccoli	0.50	corn	5.0
cow meat	0.50	soybeans	5.2
barley	0.50	sunflower seeds	5.5
tuna	0.50	rice	8.9
potatoes	0.50	torula yeast	10.
pig meat	0.50	brewer's yeast	11.
lamb	0.60	royal jelly	35.
salmon	0.80		

Pyridoxine

Pyridoxine may well be remembered as the most kicked-around of man's humble servants. We are born addicted to this vitamin; without our daily pyridoxine fix we soon need fixing. About fifty of our most important enzymes cry out for this and only this co-enzyme, every day. Fifty may not seem like a lot of enzymes when we recall that niacin flirts with over two hundred. But while niacin's enzymes mostly perform their duties with carbohydrates, pyridoxine's grease monkeys monkey around with amino acids, a much touchier subject.

With amino acids one slip of the biochemical chisel can turn a wonderful and necessary nutrient into a poison. For instance, methionine, one of the most valuable amino acids, is broken down into other things as the body uses it. As what used to be methionine is passed from enzyme to enzyme it goes through a series of changes until it finally becomes something that the body is able to get rid of without risk or trouble. It happens that a few of the enzymes involved can't function without vitamin B_6. And if any particular one of these enzymes stops functioning then the particular methionine-derived intermediate that it was supposed to degrade doesn't get degraded. One such intermediate is cystathionine. If there's no enzyme to break cystathionine down and no way to keep the stuff from coming, it starts to accumulate. And when cystathionine accumulates in the brain of a growing child, it causes mental retardation.

Another methionine intermediate is homocysteine. The enzyme that breaks it down also requires pyridoxine and when there isn't enough, homocysteine starts to accumulate. Luckily, homocysteine itself is pretty harmless, but, not so luckily, if it hangs around too long it gets converted into homocystine (we've removed an e). Homocystine, like cystathionine, also causes retardation when it gets into the workings of a growing brain. Not content with that, homocystine runs wildly through the blood supply system, damaging the walls of arteries. The cells in those walls naturally try to put something between their delicate selves and the ravaging effects of rampant homocystine molecules. They usually pick cholesterol.

Cholesterol can always be found floating around in the blood. There's plenty of it, so a little can usually be spared in an emergency. And this is an emergency. If free radicals find their way to the open wound, the chink in the vessel's armor, they'll go in and rip everything apart. Considering that there may be thousands of these chinks, one can see that the whole circulatory system could be ruined if something isn't done in a hurry.

So cholesterol begins to cover the damaged area and before long the whole thing is radical-proof and everything is fine—at least for the moment. Before long though, the area of "protection" begins to expand. This is because cholesterol is sticky; if a cholesterol molecule in the blood bumps into one that's lodged in an artery wall, they might just sit down and reminisce together for the rest of your life. Look in on them a few years later and you'll see that all their friends have dropped by to see what's going on. Other things, calcium for instance, are attracted, and anything that settles down there stays there. For the molecules involved it's a great social event, but to the person in which it happens, it's atherosclerosis.

As the years go by the cholesterol deposits widen until they cover the whole interior of the vessel; then they start to thicken. By the time the affected person gets into his later years, his blood may have a tough time squeezing through the very much narrower vessels. Meanwhile the heart has to pump a lot harder through the clogged arteries to make its presence felt in the hands and feet; the result being an overworked heart and high blood pressure. And then, the closer the vessel walls are to one another, the easier it is for clots to form inside them. Such a clot, traveling to the brain, heart or lung, is enough to kill you.

And that was only the methionine intermediates. The amino acid tryptophan has some intermediates of its own. A lack of vitamin B_6 brings out two famous ones—xanthurenic acid and hydroxy-anthranilic acid. Working together, this pair can do a lot of damage, especially to the liver. Each is at least capable of causing cancer.

Xanthurenic acid, even by itself, can make its presence regretted. Once it accumulates to a certain level, it begins to spill over into the blood stream. From here it has easy and unrestricted travel privileges to virtually any part of the body. Most of our organs find this vagabond vandal a nuisance, but one, the pancreas, is extra-sensitive to its effects.

The pancreas has a lot of functions, with different cells to carry them out. One special kind of cell has a very special job; it manufactures insulin. Without insulin, cells are unable to absorb sugar, and since sugar is their primary fuel the importance of insulin is easily understood. People with insufficient insulin-producing cells are your classic diabetics. Unless they get insulin from some other source, their cells will be forced to resort to a very inefficient fat-burning process to liberate life-sustaining energy. Before long however, the toxic by-products of this emergency measure build up to the point of seriousness, depressing the nervous system into coma and finally death.

Apparently our body's cells can't remove glucose from the blood without the help of insulin. Insulin is like the spoon that feeds them. Whenever there's a lot of sugar in the bloodstream the pancreas steps up insulin release. This shuttles some of the sugar inside the cells, the blood sugar level drops and the pancreas relaxes again.

Xanthurenic acid interferes with the absorption process. So when the blood's sugar rises and the pancreas sends out some insulin to take care of things, nothing happens. Then, when the pancreas sees the sugar level is still high it assumes, not knowing about the xanthurenic acid, that this must be new sugar. So it whips its workers into overtime to make more insulin and of course this insulin doesn't do anything either. But the insulin factory will keep trying until it drops dead from exhaustion.

That's right, dead. If something like this happens to your pancreas you get diabetes as badly and as permanently as anyone who was born with the disease. The only hope is to reverse the production of xanthurenic acid while there's still a chance for the cells of the pancreas to recuperate from their strenuous ordeal. That means restoring the missing vitamin.

Well, so far there's cancer, heart disease, diabetes and mental retardation. After all that convulsions probably won't make much of an impression but. . . .

Glutamate is normally kept in careful balance in the brain. It's balanced by GABA, (gamma-aminobutyric acid), a peaceful chemical. As long as the amount of glutamate coming in is roughly the same as that being shipped out, everything's okay. But before it's shipped out an adjustment is made on it by an enzyme that requires pyridoxine. No pyridoxine, no adjustments. After a while the glutamate starts to swamp the GABA and nasty things start happening. In fact, the adjustment we were talking about is the conversion of glutamate to GABA. So as the glutamate accumulates, the supply of new GABA is cut off and the whole balance is hopelessly upset.

Maybe that's why vitamin B_6 deficiency does what it does to the nervous system. Or maybe it's the fact that the conversion of tryptophan to serotonin requires the same vitamin. But whatever the cause, the symptoms begin with apprehension, irritability, and twitching; developing into tremors, spasms and eventually out and out epileptic-type seizures.

The frequency with which this kind of thing is seen in pregnant women has raised a lot of eyebrows, because estrogens, the female hormones, require pyridoxine for their metabolism and pregnancy greatly increases the body's production of them. This allows a person to develop a vitamin deficiency without any change in eating habits and it applies as much to people who take oral estrogens as to expectant mothers. Women take them in the form of contraceptives and men use them after prostate surgery and sex changes. Pregnancy is the most serious situation though, because a pyridoxine deficiency in Mom is very dangerous for Junior. Tough as such a condition is for an adult, it's tougher on the newborn. Among the risks are mongolism and epilepsy, fine birthday presents.

All these things happen just because some amino acid got off at the wrong exit, and so far only methionine and tryptophan, two out of twenty, have been mentioned. Another half dozen get converted to oxalate when their metabolism is interrupted, which pyridoxine deficiency can do. The oxalate is pulled out of the bloodstream by the kidney. There it meets calcium and phosphate and they all settle down together, as a kidney stone.

The key to preventing this kind of thing is to keep everything dissolved in water. Now calcium dissolves fine in the blood (which is mostly water) and so does oxalate, but the calcium salt of oxalate, calcium oxalate, does not. Instead it materializes as from nowhere, like rain precipitating from a cloud, and drops to the kidney walls. The presence of a hard granule of oxalate in the kidney acts as a magnet for the precipitation of more calcium oxalate and before you know it you've got a fair-sized rock in your system. When it gets big enough, the rock begins to roll.

Once something that big forms inside you there aren't too many ways to get it out. You can let it roll its excruciatingly painful way down the narrow passages that lead to the bladder and out, or you can visit the surgeon. As yet no convincing way of dissolving them has been found.

Normally, oxalate is pretty scarce in the urine though it is there. But B_6 deficiency can cause the level to increase enough to present real kidney stone danger. The oxalate can come not only from amino acids but from vitamin C as well. So lack of one vitamin can even make other vitamins dangerous.

And the amount of pyridoxine you need will depend on how much protein and vitamin C your body must work on, because the more work a machine has to do the faster its parts will wear out. And pyridoxine is just another part. The amino acids that really make demands though, are methionine and tryptophan. They are of course essential; with too little of them the body suffers seriously, but too much is no solution.

Animal products are excellent sources of these two amino acids, having about ten times what their vegetable counterparts can provide (though some—peanuts, wheat germ, and yeast for example—have even more than meat). One might even say that meat is too excellent a source. The problem is that meat, almost of necessity, gets cooked. And the cooking is much kinder to amino acids than to vitamins.

Whereas plants cook quickly and easily at the temperature of boiling water, animals take hours at double that temperature. When it gets this hot vitamins are being sizzled out of existence while amino acids are just enjoying the warm weather. So, though the animal originally had sufficient pyridoxine to metabolize the protein in a given amount of its tissue, the pot roast on your dinner table has a higher protein to vitamin ratio. The American inclination toward meat-centered, high-protein meals is one of the insults pyridoxine endures. Another is its price.

The cost of making an RDA's worth of pyridoxine is much higher than that of most other nutrients. This means that use of the synthetic vitamin is shied away from by industry because it raises overhead and thus cuts into profits. Profit-consciousness is not the fault of the companies that practice it, it's built into the capitalist system of economics, wherein the survival of a business depends not on how well it serves its clients but on its ability to attract profit-hungry capital, which isn't always the same thing. To our bodies all this is meaningless, since evolution has not yet provided us with an enzyme that can convert money into something that's metabolically useful. Meanwhile there is reluctance to replace the three-quarters of wheat's pyridoxine that's removed during the refining process.

There is even strong resistance to the recognition of pyridoxine as something that's indispensable to health, because such recognition would pressure the food industry to list the B_6 content of the product on its package, and that would point up how woefully deficient most commercial foods are. At present, such labelling is required only for vitamins B_1, B_2 B_3 among the Bs and A, C, iron and calcium among the rest. Of course any willful conspiracy to keep the American public blissfully unaware of the state of their nutrition is an odious crime. But there are no criminals, only victims, because people don't run the food industry, money does.

Pyridoxine also suffers through not having a big disease of it's very own, something with a scary name like pellagra or beriberi. Instead it has a lot of little diseases, most of which can also be caused by something else. This complex situation allows the forces that be to muddy the waters concerning the importance of B_6 whenever it's to their advantage. Another complication is the role of magnesium in all these diseases.

Like all the B vitamins so far discussed, pyridoxine is active only when combined with phosphate. And whenever phosphate is around, magnesium can't be too far away. But it also seems that magnesium is necessary for the pyridoxine-dependent enzymes to attach the vitamin to themselves; it seems to be the glue that binds them together. So too little magnesium results in a lot of loose pyridoxines floating around that eventually get washed away, and too little B_6 puts magnesium in the same situation. All this makes the deficiency symptoms of one tend to overlap with those of the other, and for that reason it can be pretty hard sometimes to tell which deficiency is which.

But there are now some pretty specific tests for pyridoxine deficiency that a doctor can conveniently perform. If you suspect for any reason that you have the deficiency please check with your doctor or *some* doctor, because the symptoms involved are serious, and it's important to be sure. If you don't like his advice, it's a free society and you can do what you want. Persons who should be especially attentive to this are those taking estrogens, for whatever reason, and those whose estrogen levels are naturally high due to menstruation, menopause or pregnancy. And expectant mothers should be particularly careful about using B_6 supplements. High doses during pregnancy have been known to produce children with a permanently high requirement of the vitamin.

When all this vitamin enters the fetus' ever-changing but as-yet-unformed body, it tends to think it will be born into a world of pyridoxine aplenty. So it gears its enzyme-making machinery toward the making of the pyridoxine-dependent variety. Only later does the body of the child realize that what it thought applied to the world at large really applies only to those taking vitamin supplements. But by that time the deed is done, and the child will need supplements for all the years to come.

But pregnant or not, you should make sure you have a deficiency before trying to treat it, because there's so much we have yet to understand about these things. Your doctor can check for the presence of xanthurenic acid in your urine, or he can test you for a nerve condition in the hand called the carpal tunnel syndrome. Both are considered reliable indicators of how badly you need the vitamin. Deficiencies generally take three to six weeks to develop and the same length of time to get rid of.

In the body, pyridoxine is converted mostly to pyridoxal and somewhat to pyridoxamine before attachment of the phosphate group. The -al and the -amine are the forms most often found in food and the ones most easily absorbed, but neither can be found in synthetic vitamins. Man-made B_6 is pyridoxine hydrochloride, which will also do the trick. It would be comforting to know that there was a B_6 supplement that was balanced with magnesium, but there isn't, so concerned citizens get a little less sleep at night.

Pyridoxine (mg/100 gms)

butter	0.000	pig meat	0.32
coffee	0.010	banana	0.32
honey	0.020	lamb	0.32
apples	0.030	halibut	0.34
cream	0.030	cow meat	0.40
soy lecithin	0.030	chicken	0.40
milk	0.040	oats	0.40
oysters	0.040	turkey	0.40
coconut	0.040	peanuts	0.40
mushrooms	0.050	cashews	0.40
beer	0.060	beans	0.57
fruits	0.070	shrimp	0.60
cheeses	0.080	avocadoes	0.60
clams	0.080	liver	0.67
almonds	0.100	peas	0.67
vegetables	0.15	walnuts	0.73
brazil nuts	0.17	bran	0.85
bleu cheese	0.17	tuna	0.90
pecans	0.18	wheat germ	0.92
sardines	0.18	salmon	0.98
potatoes	0.20	alfalfa	1.00
medium molasses	0.20	hazelnuts	1.1
barley	0.21	sunflower seeds	1.1
green peppers	0.26	lentils	1.7
eggs	0.27	rye	1.8
mackerel	0.27	soybeans	2.0
spinach	0.28	royal jelly	2.4
egg yolk	0.30	wheat	2.9
corn	0.30	rice	3.6
blackstrap molasses	0.31	brewer's yeast	4.0

Recommended Daily Allowances
for Pyridoxine

birth - 6 months	0.3 mg
6 months - 1 year	0.4
1 - 3 years	0.6
4 - 6 years	0.9
7 - 10 years	1.2
11 - 14	1.6
14+	2.0
pregnant women	2.5
lactating women	2.5

Cobalamin

Cobalamin and its first cousins are perhaps the most complex, non-repeating molecules to be found anywhere in nature. And there is real beauty in the structure of this very valuable vitamin. Another intriguing thing about B_{12} is that invisibly tiny amounts of it can make the difference between life and death.

Exactly what this crucial co-enzyme does in the body we seem to know, and we know what happens to people who get too little of it. But exactly how too little of it makes those things happen is still a mystery. For instance, we know it's deeply involved in the synthesis of fatty acids.

Fatty acids are just long hydrocarbon chains (fats) that have a proton stuck on one end (acids). The body builds these by hooking the carbons together two at a time, the two-carbon links being acetate. The result is a chain of sixteen or more carbons that's a lot more compact than the eight or more acetates that went into it. It can be used as membrane material or later be taken apart for use as emergency energy.

The acetate that goes into these hydrocarbonic concoctions comes from almost everywhere. It can come from the splitting of sugar molecules, the stepwise disintegration of any of several amino acids or from the reversal of fatty acid synthesis, breaking them back down into acetate. From the amino acids though, there is a complication. On the way down to the two-carbon acetate, some of the amino acids must first become a three-carbon called propionate. Three stops further down the road is an enzyme that can't work without vitamin B_{12}.

If there is a shortage of this co-enzyme, traffic gets held up and things start to accumulate in the bottleneck, all because that cobalamin-dependent enzyme can't open the gate that would let those things continue on their merry way towards becoming friendly acetates. One thing that accumulates is propionate and, since there's less acetate around and the show must go on, it soon finds itself being incorporated into fatty acids. Now, instead of getting chains with only even numbers (2, 4, 6, 8 etc.) of carbons, we're getting some odd odd-numbered chains.

Just what these new fats can do to us we don't know for sure, but we do know they don't belong. And we also know that propionate isn't supposed to hang around, it's just supposed to do its job and disappear. But we don't know how exactly all this propionate hurts us. All we know is before long nerve cells start dying. And once a nerve cell dies, that's it. It's gone—because nerve cells don't reproduce. The next step is degeneration of the spinal cord and very gradual—but irreversible—paralysis leading to death. The condition is called pernicious anemia, pernicious meaning thoroughly deadly.

Propionate only arises from four of the twenty amino acids. It also arises from the breakdown of cholesterol and odd-chain fatty acids, but there are still plenty of acetate sources that don't have propionate as an intermediate. So, once a person stops getting his B_{12}, it still takes many months for propionate to build up to toxic levels. And after that it's years till paralysis sets in. At any point along the way the whole degeneration can be stopped by supplying the vitamin, but the damage that's already been done is permanent.

Getting too little cobalamin is one way to encourage pernicious anemia, getting too much propionate would be another, but that's not easy. The body can only make it out of a few things, and relatively rare ones at that. And propionate is scarce in natural foods, so about the only way you could aggravate your chances of getting pernicious anemia would be to have a jar of propionate at the dinner table and regularly sprinkle some on your food.

But of course that's an awful lot of trouble to go through just to get something you don't want in the first place. Luckily though, you don't have to go to the trouble because the food industry does it for you. They add propionate to the great majority of baked goods "to retard spoilage", a euphemism for "to poison any molds, bacteria or other nasties that might get hungry for a slice during the long trip from the bread factory to the supermarket." Our experience with insecticides, defoliating agents, etc. has by now taught us that what's toxic to one form of life can't be too good for other forms either. At present though, next to nothing of propionate's effects on people is really known. All we can say for sure is that propionate that's eaten *is* taken into the bloodstream. Does it raise cobalamin requirements?

B_{12} is so complex a molecule that neither plants nor animals, not even the "highest" forms, have been able to de-

velop machinery sophisticated enough to make it for themselves. So from where then, does this special substance
come? The itsy-bitsy bacteria make it.

Well that makes everything clear: the bacteria in our intestines make it and we absorb it, right?

The problem is that bacteria *love* B_{12}, they need it more
than we do. If you're going to take it away from them, it'll
be over their dead little bodies, and bacteria don't start
dying until your breakfast carries them out of the small intestine, down into the large one.

So great! you say, we'll absorb it there.

The problem now is that there's only one area in the
whole digestive tract that knows how to absorb this vitamin, and it's back in the small intestine. So, as luck would
have it, the place where bacterial B_{12} becomes available is
downstream of the absorption site, and the body winds up
taking a lot of vitamin out with the rest of the garbage. It's
small wonder then that many animals (rabbits, for instance)
have taken to eating their own excrement to recapture
cobalamin.

Cows have a different solution. After a meal has digested
in the stomach for a while, a special part of its stomach
squirts some partially digested food (the cud) back into the
mouth to be chewed again. This process may go on for
hours, in the course of which a lot of bacteria will die and
liberate their B_{12}. Thus the cow gets plenty of this vitamin
and distributes it to all its cells.

So how do we get our B_{12}?

We eat the cow. Most vegetarian animals have somehow
solved the problem of getting at that bacterial B_{12} and the
ones who haven't eat the ones who have.

The fact that the human animal gets his cobalamin that
way today is often used as evidence that he never had a

vegetarian past, that he is born with the killer's meat-eating instinct. But this isn't necessarily the case. There's reason to believe that vegetables grown on manure are able to absorb substantial amounts of B_{12} from it, which people who eat those vegetables can likewise absorb.

Manure is the richest of nature's fertilizers. It's nature's way of recycling natural things for the benefit of most forms of life. Man's way is to pump his excrement into the ocean. This would make sense if algae were his staple crop, but as things stand his staple crops must settle for a distant second-best—artificial fertilizers. These spring from a belief that there's nothing that can be done that man can't do better. The more humble "organic" farmers use natural fertilizers on their crops, faithful that nature still has much to teach them.

The place where cobalamin is absorbed is at the far end of the small intestine. This means that food has to travel a goodly distance through an organ that's crammed with B_{12}-craving bacteria before it reaches safety. Without protection, the vitamin would never get there.

A lot of things happen when food is swallowed. One of them is that the stomach releases a bunch of little protein capsules that have just the right size and shape to hold a B_{12} molecule. The open capsules fumble around amid the digesting food until they happen to bump into the vitamin they were made for. And when they find their cobalamin they gobble it up and close tightly.

When doctors originally discovered how to successfully treat pernicious anemia, they realized that not one but two things were needed. One came into the body from outside and the other was already inside. Since there weren't as yet any names for these things, they were just referred to as the extrinsic factor and the intrinsic factor. The extrinsic factor is now called vitamin B_{12} and the protein overcoat is still called the intrinsic factor.

Not only is this special vitamin the only one with an escort service in the digestive tract, it also has a personal vehicle in the bloodstream. In fact, it has two different blood carrier proteins, depending on where it's going. The synthesis of *all* proteins requires plenty of amino acids and amino acids of all the many kinds. And since some foods (especially plant foods) tend to stock up on one amino acid at the expense of another, it's important to eat a varied diet. A lack of cobalamin carrier proteins causes the vitamin to be excreted and a lack of intrinsic factor will give you pernicious anemia every bit as fast as a lack of cobalamin. Maybe even faster.

It seems more than a coincidence that most pernicious anemia sufferers often have next to no stomach left at all. Others have an equally interesting feature: they destroy their own intrinsic factor.

There are lots of things the body doesn't like and most of them happen to be proteins. The poisons of snakes, spiders, scorpions, and bees are basically protein, as are the misery-inducing toxins of most disease-causing bacteria. Viruses, seen from the outside, are just big protein molecules.

Every time the body has a run-in with one of these pesky proteins, it swears to itself that it won't let it happen again. So whenever a protein-that-doesn't-belong is found in the bloodstream, we manufacture a flock of other proteins that are perfectly tailored to fit over the invading protein. These proteins are antibodies and when they run into the particular protein they're looking out for, they straightjacket him with themselves and call for help. That's the way things work when they're working right.

But put one wrench in the biochemical works and before

you know it you've got antibodies ganging up on your own intrinsic factor. This is more than a nuisance. These guys prevent cobalamin-intrinsic factor complexing on the one hand and prevent absorption of the complex on the other.

Cases like these are fortunately rare. They're most often due to stress-induced adrenal exhaustion, which in turn encourages this kind of immunological insanity. It should be remembered though, that for a goodly number of pernicious anemics cure is not just a supplement away. Some will need oral intrinsic factor, others injections. And some will get by on massive vitamin supplementation. The private citizen is best advised not to try sorting this stuff out; even doctors have trouble.

Cobalamin of food is (sorry vegies) only found in animal products. This doesn't necessarily mean meat; there's always dairy products. But beyond that there's only excrement (this vitamin isn't excreted in the urine), vegetables grown on it and putrefactive bacteria. No convenient way of eating dead putrefactive bacteria in bulk comes readily to mind, but concentrates of them are available in pill form.

Yogurt turns out to be an unreliable source of cobalamin, probably because the culture bacteria gobble it all up. It would take about ten pounds of it to supply the adult RDA, so vegetarians should look for another source. It's vegetarians, by the way, that provide us with most of our information about pernicious anemia. We thank them for their contribution to medical science, but it seems like rather a high price for them to pay. It takes several years to completely deplete liver stockpiles of cobalamin but symptoms can develop much sooner. So if you're a vegetarian and you feel the general signs of anemia, check with your doctor to see if it's pernicious. Whether it is or it isn't, you'll be glad you did.

The chief commercial form of cobalamin is cyanocobala-

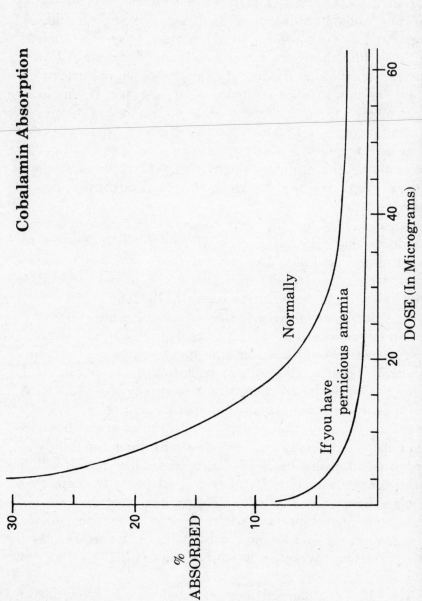

Cobalamin Absorption

Normally

If you have pernicious anemia

% ABSORBED

30

20

10

20 40 60

DOSE (In Micrograms)

NOTE: percent absorbed does the same thing with all vitamins; it falls off drastically after a certain

min and it contains cyanide. That's right, cyanide. There's not enough there to kill you; there's probably not even enough to harm you. There's just enough to make you worry, and wonder why they don't use a different form. The co-enzyme forms, methyl- and adenosyl-cobalamin, are somewhat light-sensitive and we don't want our vitamins decomposing with the first rays of dawn. But there seems to be nothing wrong with either aquo- or hydroxy-cobalamin; unless they are, God forbid, unprofitable.

There has lately been a trend towards fortifying commercial breakfast cereals with vitamins B_6 and/or B_{12}. This would be encouraging were it not for the products involved. Mostly they are grains that have been exploded ("pop" ed, "puff" ed, "crisp" ed, etc.) in such a way as to fill them with air. The temperatures required scorch the grains' vitamin content into oblivion but a few are put back. Add sugar and you've got a big, sweet box of vitamin-fortified air. A typical television ad calls them a "delicious part of any nutritious breakfast." They supply the delicious, you supply the nutritious. The pollution problem isn't such that we're reduced to buying boxes of air.

The waste involved in removing all the vitamins from their natural sources then replacing them one by one is, of course, laughably absurd; but in the case of B_{12} enrichment makes sense because it's rarely found in grains to begin with. So enriching whole-grain products with cobalamin would allow those who choose not to, not to eat animal products. The issue here is not a moral one. An acre of land used to grow soybeans can feed ten times more than one used to feed dairy cattle, and thirty times more than one used to feed beef cattle.

Cobalamin (mg/100 gm)

vegetables, fruits, oils, nuts, and yeast	0.00000000	lobster	0.0013
		liverwurst	0.0014
		sausage	0.0014
sunflower seeds	0.00000040	bleu cheese	0.0014
yogurt	0.000060	cow meat	0.0015
eggwhite	0.000090	swordfish	0.0015
butter	0.000100	muenster cheese	0.0016
cream cheese	0.00022	haddock	0.0017
buttermilk	0.00022	puffer	0.0018
cream	0.00035	eggs	0.0020
milk	0.00040	swiss cheese	0.0021
turkey	0.00042	octopus	0.0029
cod	0.00050	lamb	0.0031
chicken	0.00050	salmon	0.0047
cottage cheese	0.00059	hake	0.0049
pig meat	0.00060	squid	0.0050
anchovies	0.00062	flounder	0.0064
shrimp	0.00082	snapper	0.0088
crab	0.00085	croaker	0.0094
cheeses	0.00100	herring	0.0100
scallops	0.0011	mackerel	0.0100
egg yolk	0.0012	clam broth	0.0100
camembert	0.0012	clams	0.020
gorgonzola	0.0012	sardines	0.034
bass	0.0013	liver	0.086
halibut	0.0013		

Recommended Daily Allowances
for Cobalamin

birth - 1 year	0.3 mg
1 - 3 years	1.0
4 - 6 years	1.5
7 - 10 years	2.0
11+	3.0
pregnant women	4.0
lactating women	4.0

Folic Acid

To come down with pernicious anemia you've got to be missing two things. The more important thing is that it's pernicious; that you get from missing cobalamin. What's left is anemia, which comes from too little folic acid.

Anemia is Greek for bloodless. But it's not so much blood that anemics don't have, it's the little cells that make the blood red. We call them red cells, and they are easily the most primitive cells we have; the body's heavy laborers. All they do is pick up a load of oxygen over at one of the lungs, lug it over to some other cells, dump it, and return to the lungs for another load. This isn't exactly a fascinating job and no cell with any brains wants to spend the rest of its life doing it. But the human body, ever-resourceful, has found a solution: take their brains out.

When a red corpuscle (a.k.a. corp-suckle) is born into this world it starts out like any other; but, little does it know, it has been pre-programmed to self-lobotomize. During its period of normal growth it naturally refuses to be associated with anything as demeaning as hauling oxygen. But as time passes and its nucleus begins to shrivel to nothingness, it begins to do as it's told.

The pre-programming is built into the nucleus itself, coded in the language of the ladder-molecule, DNA. When building this ladder, the cell first builds the rungs separately (there are four different kinds) then from these loose "letters" to makes "words". The sentence sequence is next permanent-ized by locking it inside the two beams of the ladder, which is the finished DNA molecule.

One of the rungs happens to have a methyl group in it, and that must be attached while the rung is being made. But whenever you're attaching methyls you've got to have folic acid around because folic acid is the only guy that knows how to do it. Without this co-enzyme a quarter of the letters don't get made and the message gets garbled (try removing every fourth letter from the Gettysburg Address and see what you get).

As a result, the red cells don't undergo the change they were supposed to undergo. They remain intelligent enough not to want to haul oxygen and so oxygen doesn't get hauled. At the same time, less hemoglobin (the oxygen-carrying molecule) is being made, so they couldn't haul as much oxygen even if they wanted to. This brings on a state of constant and constantly worsening fatigue called anemia.

Bad as anemia is, it's not as bad as pernicious. With proper care, anemia can be made to halt, about face, and return to complete normalcy. Pernicious can be made to halt but never to retrace its steps, so any damage done up till the time of treatment is permanent.

Anemia caused by blocked DNA synthesis is the most noticeable thing that goes wrong in a folic acid deficiency, but it's not the only thing that goes wrong. With the help of folic acid the body can make three amino acids out of other things. But, without anyone to do the necessary methyl-moving, we must rely on food for our serine, histidine and methionine. And this in turn may hamper the body's protein-making abilities.

The amino acid serine, by the way, can be made by attaching a methyl group to glycine, another amino acid. Conversely, glycine can be made by removing the same methyl from serine. Now glycine also has the special job of aiding the detoxification of a relatively rare poison called benzoate. At least it used to be rare, but lately it's been showing up in some processed foods as ·a preservative. People who eat those foods are losing glycine in the form of benzoylglycine, at the rate of one molecule for every one of benzoate they absorb. This can be made up either by eating more glycine or by eating more folic acid and letting the body handle things its own way. If it's not made up then hemoglobin synthesis might be hurt, leading to a different but every bit as anemic kind of anemia. Benzoate is also suspected of causing cancer.

Food folic acid hangs around with the other members of the B complex, so wherever they can be found it can be found, but particularly so in green leaves (the word folic, like foliage, refers to leaves). The situation is complicated somewhat by other food factors that can, to greater or lesser extents, replace folic acid in the body. These things are collectively known as folacin, and, by putting the RDAs in terms of folacin, the FDA has saved us a lot of arithmetic.

While food folacin concentrations aren't particularly high, neither are requirements. Another complication, however, is that bacteria require it too, including the ones that live in our intestines and are thus in a position to share ours. Among the strains that most love folacin is *lactobacillus casei*, the one encouraged by eating cultured milk products, like yogurt. Another is *streptococcus faecalis*. Both it and *l. casei* are favored over other bacteria by high-fiber diets.

Whether or not this is really something to worry about nobody knows, for we still have much to learn about the appetites and parasitic powers of these little guys. And while we're busy finding ways to get folic acid to our cells, there's a bunch of scientists seeking better ways to keep it from them. After it was discovered that large doses of folic acid made tumors grow faster, it was only a matter of time before someone developed a drug, methotrexate, that could block cellular use of the vitamin. It has since become one of the more popular (among doctors) cancer chemotherapies. But such therapies seem like a silly waste of precious time—not for the medical profession, the medical profession makes piles and piles of money with them—but for the patient who has so little time left. This is not to say that such therapies are incapable of curing cancer (though they sometimes are) it's just that there are alternative ways of fighting cancer by strengthening the body, not weakening it. Medicine has too long ignored positive treatment concepts, such as nutrition, in favor of an all-out assault on the tumor. The problem is that while they may slow somewhat the growth of his hardy tumors, he weakens forever his body's own defenses. Disruption is what kills the patient; cancers thrive on it.

At the same time, epileptics and some schizophrenics have been found to have abnormally high amounts of folic acid in their blood. Dilantin, a drug which lowers blood folate, has been used with some success in treating convulsions in these people. It's conceivable that supplements of this vitamin would be downright dangerous for them, as they would for cancer patients.

And what about pernicious anemia? Well, a few things need straightening out here. For one thing, you can't get pernicious anemia without a B_{12} deficiency but you *can* get it without a folate deficiency. For another, a B_{12} deficiency causes both nerve damage and anemia, but a folate deficiency causes only anemia. It's also possible though, to have anemia without a deficiency of either. Thoroughly confused?

There are lots of different anemias, all caused by different things. But the kind where the red cells don't shrivel is called megaloblastic (large cell) anemia and can only be caused by B_{12} and/or folate deficiencies. So if you have a folate deficiency, you come down with this anemia. Then you take folate supplements, the anemia goes away and everything's okay.

But now suppose you have a B_{12} deficiency. You come down with the very same anemia, you think you have folate deficiency, you take extra folate, the anemia goes away and a year later you're dead. Why? Because folate, far from helping pernicious anemia, makes it more pernicious than ever.

Meanwhile all over the country people are getting this large cell anemia—an estimated 50% of America's expectant mothers have it. These people mostly have folate deficiencies and they need folate or they won't get better. But the doctors don't know what to do because they might have B_{12} deficiencies.

It also makes a problem for the FDA. Is it safe to let folic acid supplements float around freely considering that so many people could harm themselves by taking them and that even doctors are baffled by the intricacies of megaloblastic anemia? It was finally decided that no pill can have contain more 0.4 milligrams of this vitamin if it's going without prescription. Pregnant women can buy 0.8 mg tablets and as much as 1.5 mg per pill is available by prescription. This restriction makes it tougher for a lot of people with folate deficiency to get better in the hope that a few will be spared irreversible nerve damage. It was a hard decision to make and it seems like the right one, but I'm glad I didn't have to make it.

Folacin (mg/100 gm)

tuna	0.0010	almonds	0.050
egg white	0.0010	brazil nuts	0.050
shrimp	0.0020	broccoli	0.050
lamb	0.0030	brussel sprouts	0.050
clams	0.0030	corn	0.059
pig meat	0.0030	greens	0.060
carrots	0.0080	walnuts	0.060
human milk	0.0100	soy lecithin	0.060
medium molasses	0.010	peanuts	0.060
potatoes	0.010	kale	0.070
radishes	0.010	hazelnuts	0.070
turkey	0.010	spinach	0.080
green peppers	0.010	collard greens	0.100
cheeses	0.010	sunflower seeds	0.10
fruits	0.010	green peas	0.11
salmon	0.011	asparagus	0.12
cow milk	0.011	sprouts	0.14
egg yolk	0.013	rice	0.17
vegetables	0.020	barley	0.21
mushrooms	0.020	wheat	0.22
halibut	0.020	split peas	0.23
cream	0.020	liver	0.29
cashews	0.025	wheat germ	0.31
bananas	0.030	beans	0.31
coconut	0.030	lentils	0.34
eggs	0.030	oats	0.39
sardines	0.030	chickpeas	0.41
cottage cheese	0.030	endive	0.47
pecans	0.030	soybeans	0.69
rye	0.035	alfalfa	0.80
bran	0.040	brewer's yeast	2.0
cow meat	0.040	torula yeast	3.0

Recommended Daily Allowances
for Folacin*

birth - 1 year	50 micrograms
1 - 3 years	100 mcg
4 - 6 years	200
7 - 10 years	300
11+	400
pregnant women	800
lactating women	600

* If there's a gram of something in food that has folic acid properties but is only a tenth as potent, it would be lying to say that there's a tenth of a gram of folic acid in there. Instead we say that there's a tenth of a gram of "folacin", an imaginary substance whose potency would equal folic acids.

Biotin

Here's a vitamin that starts to stretch the definition of vitamin. The whole concept of a vitamin is based on scarcity and our whole interest in the subject is that if we don't watch out we'll come down with some disgusting disease. Well here's a vitamin that nobody gets deficiencies of.

Biotin too is a co-enzyme. It's specialty is moving carbon dioxide (one carbon, two oxygens) groups from one molecule to another. There are at least six enzymes that use biotin in this capacity, one of them being in the same assembly line for propionate breakdown that B_{12} attends. So a biotin deficiency presumably could lead to pernicious nerve damage, if there was any such thing as a biotin deficiency. If you use enough saccharin however, you might not need a biotin deficiency to get this disease, because saccharin inhibits the operation of this enzyme.

There's a lot of biotin in food but it's not like there's so much that it's impossible not to get the half a milligram or so per day that's recommended. Added to which is the fact that food processing removes or destroys a large percentage of what the food started out with. So how come there aren't more biotin deficiencies?

The most likely explanation is that our intestinal bacteria are helping us out with this vitamin, and it's probably true. In that event, one way to get a deficiency is to murder all your bowel buddies, your faecal friends. This you could do with oral antibiotics. Antibiotics (meaning literally "anti-life") aren't particular about what they kill—take enough of them and they'll kill you too—so by taking them regularly, you can eventually reduce the population of your intestinal intimates to zero and keep it there. Then, if you maintain yourself on junk food, you might just get yourself a genuine biotin deficiency.

There is a protein called avidin that has a strong affinity for biotin. Perhaps it's an enzyme complex that needs biotin as co-enzyme. Anyway, it binds the biotin very tightly to itself and is too large for our intestines to absorb, so our biotin will just pass on through with the avidin. This avidin stuff could present a serious problem but for the fact that only one food, the whites of egg, contains it. And even here, avidin is easily destroyed by cooking. But every so often the medical journals report that some weirdo has been eating nothing but raw eggs for the past twenty years and has finally come down with a biotin deficiency. Serves him right.

Biotin (mg/100 gm)

soy lecithin	0.00	eggs	0.020
potatoes	0.00010	wheat germ	0.020
apples	0.0010	clams	0.020
human milk	0.0010	mackerel	0.020
fruits	0.0025	corn	0.021
cheeses	0.0036	sardines	0.024
cow meat	0.0040	oats	0.024
yams	0.0043	wheat	0.027
bananas	0.0044	pecans	0.030
cow milk	0.0047	cashews	0.030
vegetables	0.0050	tuna	0.030
avocadoes	0.0060	alfalfa	0.030
pig meat	0.0062	barley	0.031
goat's milk	0.0063	chickpeas	0.032
eggwhite	0.0070	peanuts	0.040
sprouts	0.0080	walnuts	0.040
halibut	0.0080	lentils	0.042
oysters	0.0087	green peas	0.042
shrimp	0.010	egg yolk	0.052
turkey	0.010	rice germ	0.058
medium molasses	0.010	rice bran	0.060
lamb	0.010	rice	0.070
coconut	0.010	sunflower seeds	0.070
chicken	0.011	split peas	0.082
bran	0.014	butter	0.100
salmon	0.015	torula yeast	0.10
mushrooms	0.016	liver	0.12
cauliflower	0.017	soybeans	0.19
beans	0.017	brewer's yeast	0.20
almonds	0.018	royal jelly	0.29
bee pollen	0.020	rye	0.33
blackstrap molasses	0.020		

Lipoic Acid

Here at last is a vitamin that takes care of itself; we don't have to do anything. It's found in lots of foods, but we don't have to worry about which ones or how much they contain. Our intestinal bacteria probably don't supply us with any, but it doesn't matter. It's a co-enzyme in the critical conversion of glucose to acetate and if our cells didn't have it, it would probably be a catastrophe, but we won't let ourselves be bothered about that—because this is one co-enzyme that the body can make for itself.

Lipoic acid is not available in supplement form, nor is there as yet any reason why it should be. Scientists of the future will doubtless discover nutritional factors that are associated with either the synthesis or use of lipoic acid. That will give the people of the future something new to worry about.

To give you an idea of what's in food: 100 gms of wheat germ contains 7.3 mg of lipoic acid.

Choline

A lot of what happens in the body depends on shape. Different molecules always have different shapes. Knowing this, the body has made a lot of gates that only molecules of a very specific shape can fit through. Thus, by putting molecules through processes that change their shape, our cells can control the power of those molecules—if they can't get to where they're going, they obviously can't do anything when they get there. This trick can reduce a powerful molecule to impotence.

One of the simplest (and therefore most popular) ways to change a molecule's shape is to add or subtract little one-carbon methyl groups. This small alteration can make poisons harmless or innocuous substances into very influential ones. But in order to do all these things the body's got to have a supply of methyl groups.

All jobs of this nature tend to fall on the liver. If the liver's really in a jam it can make its own methyls with the help of a folic acid enzyme and some amino acids, but most of the time the liver is much too busy to take time out for methyl manufacture. And besides, why should it when there are plenty of methyls in food?

Every time you eat a choline molecule, you supply your liver with three methyl groups to do with as it sees fit. This is more than a convenience though: through the course of millions of years of evolution there has always been plenty of choline in the diet and the liver has come to rely on it. If our species wants to replace choline-rich foods with refined grains, sugar-candy and alcohol and expects the liver to get used to that, we've got a few million years of waiting ahead of us.

In the meantime, our liver reacts to choline deficiency with an emergency overhaul of its enzyme systems. This state of affairs can hold out for quite a while, a few years perhaps, but then the liver starts to degenerate. First it starts to swell with fat, but the expansion quickly levels off and shrinkage begins as the fat is gradually replaced by blood, pus and finally cartilage. When all you have left is a shriveled mass of knotted cartilage it's called cirrhosis of the liver. But it's not a liver any more and that shrunken lump never again will be one. Considering the wide range of wonderful things the liver can do, it seems like a good organ not to be without. But methyl-donation is only one side of the body's use of choline. It can, for instance, be combined with acetate to form acetylcholine.

All actions start out as thoughts. After the brain has stewed enough about the things it would like, it decides on an appropriate way to make them happen and starts sending out signals to the appropriate muscles. The signals are sent out of the brain, which is made up of nerve cells, and passed from nerve cell to nerve cell. All this goes smoothly since nerve cells understand other nerve cells pretty well.

You might say that the message gets from one end to the other because everyone in between speaks the same language.

But muscle cells speak a different language and without an interpreter they can't understand what it is they're supposed to do. Acetylcholine is the interpreter: it carries the message from the last nerve cell on the relay chain, across a little gap called a synapse, and over to the muscle cell. Acetylcholine explains to the muscle cell that Brain has something in mind and would really appreciate it if that particular muscle cell could see its way clear to contract. Once the muscle cell understands this, it's only too happy to co-operate and does whatever it can to help.

A deficiency of choline sooner or later means a deficiency of acetylcholine. This in turn brings on fatigue and muscle damage. In the kidney, the reaction is release of a hormone called vasopressin, which elevates blood pressure. Persistently high blood pressure starts to damage the blood vessels, fat collects in the damaged areas and further increases the blood pressure by reducing vessel diameter, and pretty soon you've got a nice case of circulatory disease. The kidney is very sensitive to this kind of thing. The heart is too, complicated by the fact that, being a muscle, it also needs acetylcholine to function.

The body actually does though, have a defense mechanism against the buildup of fat and cholesterol in its arteries. It's something called lecithin, which does for the bloodstream what bile does for digesting food: it emulsifies big fat bubbles into tiny ones. Thus can lecithin break up fat deposits that have already precipitated onto artery walls. Lecithin then could be very helpful against the circulatory complications of either choline or pyridoxine deficiencies. But, as luck would have it, the liver uses a pyridoxine-dependent enzyme in the making of lecithin and choline turns out to be a vital lecithin ingredient.

It's not only in the circulatory system that one runs into circular problems like this. It can also be seen in the drugs that sick people take; for they most often replace an obvious sickness with a subtler, more insidious one. Taking drugs has become a disease in itself, and experience shows time and again that the things the body best accommodates are food, its derivatives, and oxygen. With anything else second best tends to be the very best one can hope for. And second best can often be terrible.

Choline is another of the magically medicinal molecules that food contains, and food contains quite a lot of it. There's so much in fact, that getting a less than adequate amount would seem impossible. The problem is that only a few per cent of eaten choline ever gets to be absorbed choline, thanks to the action of intestinal bacteria. Exactly what the percentage is depends on what kind of bacteria they are. And what kind of bacteria they are depends on what kind of food you eat. Some bacteria like meat, some like vegetables, others like coffee and doughnuts. Inside a coffee and doughnuts eater the coffee-and-doughnuts bacteria will thrive while the others pack up and go to another restaurant. Some day we may know enough about this subject to use food selection to steer bacterial populations in the direction of our choosing, say, to eliminate the choline consumers. But until then we'll have to read our vitamin labels with care.

There seem to be a few vitamin companies that haven't heard the news about choline non-absorption. Accordingly, their multi-vitamins contain choline and, for instance, thiamin in about the same amounts. Even the bacteria would be disappointed by this. More conscientious companies provide choline and thiamin in a ratio of about ten to one, expecting 90% of the choline to be ambushed by bacteria. This number may be realistic, it may not—it's just a guess. Our food, however, has a choline-to-thiamin ratio of about 500.

Maybe nature is trying to tell us something.

But even if there were no such thing as choline, the situation wouldn't necessarily be hopeless, because our bodies have developed a way of making an emergency supply from the amino acid serine should the need arise. Serine, however, has other jobs to do that are of equal importance, so a serine surplus from a high-protein diet is a pre-requisite for choline creation. And of course we can save our bodies some sweat and serine by just eating the finished product— choline.

Before choline can be prevailed upon to donate its methyl groups for the worthy cause of keeping us alive, the liver must first convert it to something called betaine (that's three syllables). That means we could short-cut the process by providing our systems with betaine, directly. And it happens that beets (Latin for beet is beta) are stocked with the stuff. The problem is that betaine can't be converted to either lecithin or acetylcholine. The amino acid methionine can also supply methyl groups, but for this purpose it's even less useful than betaine.

It's not that it's impossible for us ever to improve on nature's recipe for good health—food, that is, and in nature's form—it's just that to beat nature you have to really understand nature. This is something science is only just beginning to do, and something the food industry hasn't even tried to do. So don't think there's no room for imagination in the field of nutrition, because the real miracles will come when we really comprehend the workings of our bodies. Wait and see.

Choline (mg/100 gm)			
apples	1.0	bran	140
eggwhite	2.0	alfalfa	140
vegetable oils	5.0	blackstrap molasses	150
fruits	10	sprouts	210
yams	12	sunflower seeds	220
milk	15	brewer's yeast	240
cheeses	50	peanuts	240
pecans	50	spinach	240
cow meat	70	torula yeast	250
corn	71	cabbage	250
trout	87	green peas	270
wheat	92	green beans	340
corn	92	soybeans	340
oats	94	wheat germ	400
carrots	95	eggs	500
vegetables	100	caviar	540
veal	100	liver	550
potatoes	110	rice	650
flax seeds	110	split peas	700
lamb	110	lentils	710
pig meat	120	chickpeas	780
asparagus	130	egg yolk	1700
barley	140	soy lecithin	2900

Inositol

Lecithin is basically fatty acids, but fatty acids alone can't do what lecithin does. Its critical emulsifying ability is in part due to the small (3%) but essential amount of choline it contains. And the same is true of inositol.

Together, in the same amounts and combined with phosphate, these biochemical brothers allow lecithin to stand guard over fat bubbles in the bloodstream, keeping them small, divided and under control. The bigger they are, the sooner they bump against vessel walls and begin atherosclerotic accumulation. Lecithin not only counter-acts this, but is also a key constituent of myelin, the nerve insulator. Deficiencies could therefore induce jangled nerves and insomnia.

Inositol can be found in any natural food source, animal or vegetable, and usually in quantities closely matching those of choline. A really concentrated source is purified lecithin, which comes as both granules and liquid in our stores. It's usually from soybeans, but lecithin is lecithin, wherever it comes from.

Any estimate of the inositol in a plant probably counts inositol hexaphosphate too, which might not be such a good idea. Inositol hexaphosphate, also known as phytic acid, may contain inositol, but that won't do us any good because we can't absorb it. It may even be detrimental.

Biochemists talk about things called inositols, but only one of these is the inositol we're talking about. That one they call myo-inositol. The differences between biochemists and other people don't go much further.

Inositol (mg/100 gm)

halibut	17	cantaloupe	120
salmon	18	strawberries	120
eggs	22	sunflower seeds	150
cheeses	25	grapefruit	150
potatoes	29	peas	160
vegetables	30	wheat	170
apples	31	blackstrap molasses	170
oysters	44	peanuts	180
turnip greens	46	alfalfa	210
chicken	48	oranges	210
carrots	48	beans	240
tomatoes	50	cow meat	260
corn	50	torula yeast	270
cow's milk	50	oats	320
brewer's yeast	50	liver	340
lettuce	55	veal	340
lamb	57	barley	390
watermelon	64	pig meat	410
yams	66	lentils	410
sprouts	70	wheat germ	690
fruits	80	rice	700
human milk	92	chickpeas	760
cabbage	95	tea leaves	1000
cauliflower	95	soy lecithin	2100

Pangamic Acid

The people who brought you sputnik, kirlian photography and hands that read books now bring you a new vitamin, sometimes calles B_{15}. And like the other Soviet brainstorms this one may be a bit hard for us to take at first.

Another thing that makes it hard to take is that it's not yet generally available in pill form. The idea of something being unavailable is always discomforting, even if you're not sure you need it—and in this case it's not clear that you do. There's reason to believe that pangamate somehow increases the efficiency of our oxygen transport. But then there's reason not to believe it too. Until the majority makes up its mind, the individual will have to make up his for himself.

Pangamic acid is a fusion of glucuronic acid and something called dimethyl-glycine. And it happens that dimethyl-glycine is also in that choline-betaine-methyl sequence; in fact it's further down the road than choline or betaine, though it should, theoretically, be less useful than either. At any rate, dimethyl-glycine seems to be the active ingredient of pangamate and one can see how it might be a nice thing for your liver to have.

This new nutrient has been recommended for athletes and anemics, generally in amounts of hundreds of milligrams per day. If you want it and can't find it in stores, food is still your friend. The search for this nutrient in food is just beginning and as yet, few numbers are in. It should prove plentiful though, since glycine is a fairly common amino acid and methyl groups abound in nature. Here's the first taste of what's to come: 100 grams of wheat germ contains 31 mg of B_{15}. The following table shows relative amounts of B_{15} for various grains.

barley	12 mg
corn	150
oats	110
wheat germ	70
and rice bran	200

Amygdalin

Seeds are a very rich source of practically every known nutrient. Yet animals seem to avoid, for some rason, eating fertilized seeds (those found in fruits). Among the things they contain is vitamin B_{17}. And that may be why animals avoid them.

As yet the only use found for amygdalin is killing things, and even this it does with debatable effectiveness. Considering that this poison is found in some very popular foods, you may be wondering why you haven't heard of it sooner. But you've probably heard of cyanide. Tiny cyanide molecules have an incredible ability to block the action of an enzyme that's critical to food combustion in each of the body's trillions of cells. If there are enough cyanide molecules, death will occur in a couple of minutes. Without the cyanide it contains, amygdalin would be harmless and most likely of no use to us at all. But as things stand, we can try and put it to work against one of our most formidable enemies.

It turns out that cancer cells have been provided by nature with an enzyme that releases the cyanide from amygdalin, and very efficiently too. By a tantalizing coincidence, normal cells don't have that enzyme. Perhaps, with amygdalin in the bloodstream, cancer cells will unlock Pandora's box with their enzyme and be strangled by cyanide as the good guys look smugly on.

Perhaps. But it doesn't look that way. Reports from Europe, Mexico, etc. indicate that, under the name Laetrile, amygdalin can relieve cancer pain and once in a while slow or stop the growth of a tumor. These reports come from outside the U.S. because the American Medical Association has thrown its political weight behind having the "drug" banned here (although some state legislatures have overturned this). If this is because of its potential danger, why shouldn't the same physicians who use curare and nitroglycerine be trusted with Laetrile? If it's because the drug doesn't cure cancer then everything in this country should be banned.

As yet though, there's no law against eating fruit seeds. But don't think that not having that enzyme is insurance against cyanide poisoning; the cyanide can be liberated in other ways and some gets liberated anyway. One fellow killed himself with one cup of raw apple seeds. Cooking, soaking or otherwise fooling around with the seeds can make them much more dangerous. Symptoms of cyanide poisoning start with headache, nausea, numbness and chest tightness ending in convulsions and death. Maybe the numbness is related to the pain relief.

If you're wondering why anything as dangerous and nutritionally unnecessary as amygdalin would be called a vitamin, you are not alone.

B$_{17}$ (mg/100 gm)

When people talk about vitamin B$_{17}$ they usually mean not only amygdalin but also the nitriles, the nitrilosides and all the other organic cyanide complexes plants contain. Our numbers will do the same, except for the almonds, for which the amount of pure amygdalin is given. 300 mg per day is considered a normal, healthy dose while cancer patients are generally advised to get 3000 with a ceiling of 20,000. Any dose that produces nausea is considered borderline, not to be exceeded. When given by injection however, almost any dose seems safe.

mature almonds	15	quince seeds	680
young almonds	30	flax seeds	900
black-eyed peas	34	bitter cassava	940
navy beans	34	wild cherry bark	1300
kidney beans	34	green lima beans (Java)	1700
white limas (U.S.)	170	bean sprouts	2000
guava seeds	190	white limas (Burma)	3600
vetch	310	bitter almonds	4200
buckwheat	340	black limas (Puerto Rico)	5100

Para-aminobenzoic Acid

This is a vitamin that's part of another vitamin. Para-aminobenzoic acid (PABA) combined with glutamate and pteridine is folic acid. Folic acid we know is important; the question is whether PABA can do anything on its own. The FDA is pretty sure it can't, so sure in fact that they've made it illegal for vitamin manufacturers to claim otherwise. But there's hard evidence that it can.

Bacteria do need PABA; that much everyone admits. Without it they shrivel up and die pretty quickly. Fifty or so years ago somebody replaced PABA's carboxyl group with a different one containing sulfur and fed the result to some bacteria. The new compound was similar enough for them to gobble it up greedily, but different enough to be of no use once it was absorbed. So, as the cell suffers from an ever-worsening PABA deficiency, it doesn't bother to eat any more PABA because it thinks it's already got plenty.

The problem with sulfa antibiotics is that our cells aren't really any smarter than bacteria; it's just that, having a different metabolism, our cells take longer to develop and ex-

pire from a PABA deficiency. But when they do, you hear
about it—in the form of anemia, depression and diarrhea. It
might be possible to survive in this condition, but it certainly wouldn't be fun.

Food PABA tends to outnumber food folic acid about
twenty to one (further indication that the body does more
with it than make folate) so deficiency really shouldn't be a
problem. Food, however, supplies only a tenth of what's
being recommended against sunburn these days.

Photons of ultraviolet light, more energetic than any in
the visible range, have enough power to knock loose rungs
in the DNA ladder or to convert harmless molecules into
free radicals that can do the job for them. If you're lucky,
the cells will just die and be done with it; enough dead cells
adding up to a case of sunburn. But better a burn than
cancer.

PABA seems either to absorb ultraviolet directly or,
through its anti-oxidant properties, to prevent free radical
production in the skin. Free radicals may also be responsible for the formation of hard, brittle skin. They could do so
by attacking molecules of a protein called keratin.

On their own, keratin molecules are soft and docile. But
all of them have sulfur atoms that are very lonely for one
another. If they could, they'd reach out to each other and
hold on for dear life, but they can't. All the sulfur atoms in
keratin have individual hydrogen watch-dogs attached to
them that stand between the sulfurs. Then, if a free radical
comes along and bumps off the molecular chastity belts, the
hydrogens, the sulfur atoms can dash together and pretty
soon all the keratin molecules become intertwined, held together by the sulfur-sulfur bonds. This is what makes tough
skin tough. Protein cross-linking like this is responsible for
many of the symptoms of old age, both in the skin and

elsewhere. If PABA can be of any use in this department, the people of the world want to know about it.

Some food values (few have been tested):
(mg/100 gm)

wheat germ 0.037

brewer's yeast 0.49

liver 0.62

sunflower seeds 62.

Carnitine

The body makes its own carnitine and it's only once in a blue and yellow polka-dotted moon that anything like a carnitine deficiency develops, unless you're a mealworm. It's used as a carrier of finished fatty acids out of the mitochondrion where they are made, and of acetates into the mitochondrion where they get strung together to make fatty acids. This kind of thing happens an awful lot in muscle cells so meat is the best food source of carnitine (from the Latin *carnis* which means flesh). Plant products also have some, maybe about 1% of what meat does.

Carnitine in purified form hasn't yet found a following in the bottled health market. Used clinically, it causes pupil dilation, mouth watering, and diarrhea. Carnitine also goes by the name of vitamin B_T, T for *tenebrio molitor* which is Latin for mealworm.

Insects, it turns out, can't grow without carnitine in their diet and have to go out and get some every day. Next time you see an insect, remember he's got problems too.

In food:

(mg/100 gm)			
wheat	1.0	yeasts	2.5
alfalfa	2.0	fishes	70.

Ascorbic Acid

This is the vitamin that has everyone excited, optimistic and thoroughly confused—and nowhere is this more true than with the scientists, the very people we look to for reliable and coldly objective facts. So far, vitamin C has been recommended to combat cancer, atherosclerosis, every viral disease, every bacterial disease, poisoning of all kinds, mental illness, injury, temperature extremes, old age, diabetes, allergy, cataracts, kidney stones, radiation sickness, arthritis, headaches and bee stings. Now really, what else is there?

And meanwhile, on the other side of the C-saw, there are those who claim that those who buy supplements of the vitamin could as well be throwing their money in a wishing well. Somewhere between must lie the truth.

A molecule of vitamin C is small and simple and rather resembles a sugar. Thanks to this and its ability to dissolve in water, the vitamin finds its way into many a remote bodily corner. And once it gets there it *could* do almost anything because it's a very reactive molecule. This theoretical possibility explains the number and variety of claims that have been made for it. Some of these claims have been tested and proven, one of them being the importance of ascorbic acid in hydroxylation reactions.

Hydroxylation means tacking a hydroxyl (OH) group onto some molecule or other. That vitamin C should turn out to be involved in this sort of thing makes sense because it happens to have two very restless hydroxyls of its own. What a hydroxyl does to the thing it's added to depends on which thing it's added to.

There are, for instance, two amino acids, proline and lysine, that can be hydroxylated to form two new amino acids, hydroxyproline and hydroxylysine. These guys have only one use in the body but it's worth remembering: they are key ingredients in the recipe for a protein called collagen. Collagen makes use of the hydroxyls to set up very tight bonds with other collagen molecules. And this tight binding makes collagen a remarkably tough and flexible material. The body is then able to use it in structures that need strong support but where bone would be too rigid.

This protein is generated by small spider-like cells called fibroblasts which move around in the old collagen weaving webs of new collagen. Continuous replacement ensures lifelong strength and resilience for the many tissues that depend on it for support. But without vitamin C, the old collagen will be replaced with mush.

The fibroblasts do the proline and lysine hydroxylations for themselves and then string the new amino acids together with others, making collagen. If those hydroxylations don't get done, the fibroblast continues as though they had been, putting ordinary proline and lysine into its protein lengths. The result is a different protein that resembles collagen but will never do as a substitute. Lacking hydroxyl groups, its molecules slip and slide over one another, the tightly-knit fabric begins to come apart at the seams, and the whole structure begins to disintegrate. With this leg kicked out from under them, blood vessels start to slouch, becoming flabby and undisciplined. In this condition even a slight jolt can cause them to burst, and dump their purple cargo under the skin in the form of a bruise. The muscles become fragile and lethargic. Little pains shoot up from dozens of different places. If the situation continues, the body will degenerate into a bleeding pulp for which death is a blessing. This is scurvy.

To keep this kind of thing from happening to them, land animals had to have a reliable source of ascorbic acid. (Ascorbic means against scurvy). Plants made their own and did so in quantities sufficient to keep the plant-eating animals happy. And as long as the plant eaters were well-supplied the animals that ate them were too.

The only problem was that C was such a reactive substance that only the careful compartmentalization of the living cell can keep it out of trouble. So when a plant or animal dies its ascorbate is quickly oxidized by the flood of protoplasmic potpourri that pours from the decaying cells. In order to have any value as a C source, food must be fresh, very fresh.

This seems pretty acceptable until you consider what happens to the poor plant-eaters. In the summertime the living is easy: there's plenty of green grass, fresh leaves, ripe fruits—all of them fine C sources. But once a year comes winter, and the end of all those things. And if the rabbits can't get it from the plants, the wolves can't get it from the rabbits.

One possible solution would be to store summer C in the body till winter. With a fat-soluble vitamin you can get away with such prolonged storage but in water things happen much much faster and you can't. C is water soluble.

The other possibility was to make C in the body out of something that was available year-round. The something turned out to be glucose, which can be converted to C in five easy steps. For these five steps five new enzymes were needed, which meant five new blueprints in the DNA molecule.

The ability to make its own ascorbic acid also gave the animal control over how much it could get in a given situation. And it happens that one of C's jobs follows a completely unpredictable schedule. Unlike the sun's rhythmic rising and setting, the monthly march of the moon or the imperceptible progression of the seasons through a year, many events won't fit into a pattern. The body can't know in advance when an injury will occur, a disease strike or the food supply run short. For stressful situations like these the body must simply be ready.

The liver, kidneys and adrenal glands are all rich in an enzyme called cytochrome P-450, a key link in the electron transport chain for those organs. This chain provides them with the bulk of their energy, the energy that performs their invaluable functions. But cytochrome P-450 is a hydroxylating enzyme, one that requires vitamin C.

In times of stress the energy needs of the liver and kidneys will increase, but those of the adrenals will skyrocket. It's the adrenals after all that make the stress hormones; during the crisis they release their stored steroids and have to work overtime replacing them. If the emergency continues, they'll have to work twice as hard. And unless the vitamin C supply keeps pace with the vitamin C demand, the glands will ruin themselves with their task.

A similar, but less drastic situation exists in the liver, where dozens of the most common poisons are sent for (hopeful) detoxification. Frequently the detoxification is by direct hydroxylation. In other cases the hydroxyl serves as a handle for the attachment of a sugar molecule. This makes the poison more water-soluble, making hard-to-get-rid-of molecules easier for the kidney to handle.

In all these cases the body is able to meet especially trying experiences with appropriately high amounts of vitamin C, as long as it's making its own. And there aren't too many things that can prevent it from doing so, but there are a few. For example, what if something should happen to those blueprints in the DNA molecule? If something changes the plan for an enzyme, the cell will put the amino acids in the wrong order when building that enzyme. The odds are strongly against such a defective enzyme being able to do its job.

To make a change in our DNA all it takes is for one of the zillions of cosmic rays whistling through us every second, for just one of them to smack into the molecule in exactly the right way, so as to knock one of the rungs out of the ladder or maybe change one rung into another. There are also chemicals that are very good at this sort of thing, including caffeine, saccharin, artificial food colors and most of your proven cancer-causers. Normally when this happens the cell will just die, or live on in some crazy way until the animal itself dies, when the cell will die with it. The interesting things happen when the defect (or, rarely, the improvement) somehow gets passed on to the next generation. This can only happen if the cosmic ray or whatever hits one of the germ cells found down in the ovaries or testicles, and even then only if that particular cell happens to be the one chosen for fertilization and even *then* only if the creature that results is able to survive long enough to reproduce and pass the change on to the next generation. Et cetera!

Well the blueprints for the enzymes that convert glucose

to C, or at least one of them, must be in a very vulnerable position on the DNA molecule because mishaps with them seem to be very common. But of course, most of the victims of this biochemical boo-boo don't live to tell about it. The only way they could is if they happened to eat lots of fruits and berries (the richest C sources) and to live in places where there was plenty of that kind of thing around, jungles for instance.

The red-vented bulbul, a bird that favors the more tropical areas of India, depends on its food for ascorbic acid, as does the Indian fruit-eating bat. The guinea pig, hailing from the lush island of New Guinea, is in the same situation. And so are the great apes. In fact, all things considered, one would be surprised if it didn't happen to the great apes. They are so carefully designed for living in trees (and that's where the fruits are) that they'd be silly to even think of leaving the jungle, so why shouldn't they drop the burden of making something that will always be in their food? But then no one guessed that one of them would get smart.

When the first humans ventured out of the jungle to see what lay beyond the horizon they didn't know how much they were leaving behind. The cave men, like today's eskimos, didn't know why it was that unless they ate their meat raw they would die a gruesome death. It took no doubt thousands of years and millions of such deaths to establish the social and cultural traditions that protected our ancestors from scurvy.

But then along came the Age of Reason and man could safely forget the dark preachings of the witch doctor in the cold clear light of knowledge. So off they went on months-long sea voyages well-stocked with preserved food, and they succumbed by the scores to scurvy, an all but forgotten disease.

Twentieth-century science has, in this respect at least, caught up with the medicine man: we now know that cooking and prolonged storage give a vitamin that doesn't like being itself the opportunity to change into something else, and *nothing* else will prevent scurvy. The problem is that since there were no scientists around to take measurements when our remote ancestors were making their own vitamin C, we really don't know how much our body wants for itself. We can get a rough idea from the lucky creatures that can make C, by seeing how much they make.

C Synthesis in Animals

Toads don't make that much vitamin C in a day, but then toads don't have nearly as many cells as we do. People weigh in at about sixty kilograms each. So, on a per cell basis . . .

A 60 kg toad would make for himself about 11 gms daily.

60 kg frog	9
turtle	7½
goat	5
cow	4
mouse	3
rabbit	2
and a 60 kg cat	½

One thing we see is that different animals feel they need different amounts, and the amounts they feel they need will jump five times or so in times of stress.

You see, that's the problem. Stress situations happen suddenly—if you're being chased by a lion you'd like your liver to respond by making and releasing more C while you're on the run. Instead, nature seems to expect us to stop and consume a crate of oranges before proceeding further.

Well technology has whittled the crate of oranges down to a couple of pills for us, but problems remain. We still don't know how much to take or exactly when to take it.

We could try taking a really big dose every day or so but then a new problem arises—tolerance. If the body gets used to having big C doses as a matter of course, it seems to get lazy. Maybe the body decides that with all this ascorbate around it can afford to make more cytochrome P-450 and rely on it even more than before for energy. So when an emergency comes up and the same old big C dose comes down the pipe, the adrenals say "So what else is new?" They need more.

The same thing would happen to C-making creatures if stress-stimulated C doses hung around in the body for a while—they might get used to them. So their kidneys are designed to get rid of it with all haste once the crisis has passed, and this is good. But now take a look at us. A small change in our DNA has deprived our livers of the ability to make the enzymes that make ascorbic acid, but it hasn't affected our kidneys. Our kidneys seem to think we still make our own ascorbate and there will always be plenty more where the stuff that's around at the moment came from, so they too get rid of it with all haste once the crisis has passed. This is not good.

It means that man is at an evolutionary crossroads. Under normal circumstances, nature would have to decide whether to restore our C-making powers or make changes that would allow us to store this necessary nutrient more efficiently. But nature doesn't just look at the alternatives and choose the one that's most promising, nature wants to try out *all* the alternatives and let them slug it out in the environmental arena for a million years or so to see who comes up winner.

In that way of doing things it doesn't matter how many losers there are as long as there is a winner. In the face of this cruel system it's natural for man to seek a solution that's more considerate of his own kind. Accordingly, scientists are looking to something called recombinant gene research to gain an understanding of our own DNA molecule, its assets and its liabilities. Such an understanding, used properly, could allow us to repair our own chromosomes. And through our chromosomes one generation can achieve what would otherwise have required eons of haphazard mutation and natural selection. All the hereditary diseases could be eradicated, among them hemophilia, sickle-cell anemia and diabetes, not to mention the disease we've all inherited, vitamin C addiction.

To prevent scurvy, a daily ascorbate "fix" of 60 milligrams is recommended. Those who would follow this recommendation however, should consider that their cells would be getting less ascorbate than those of any other land animal. We've seen how much those who can make it make for themselves, but even those who can't (our species excepted) don't take chances with their health. A gorilla, for instance, eats a good five grams' worth every day, and he eats them continuously. That means his blood has a relatively constant level of vitamin C in it.

We, on the other hand, tend to let our hunger build for hours and then gorge ourselves. This may be fine for social decorum and it does keep food-garbage out of our workshops, but it's pretty rough on the body. Our regimented eating habits cause blood levels of ascorbate (and just about everything else too) to rise drastically during the first couple of hours after a meal and then to fall just as drastically as time goes on. It's small wonder that people are so moody.

But meals at least happen about three times a day, while vitamin supplements usually come once. Within six hours after taking a C supplement the blood C level is back where it started, thanks to the efficient work of our kidneys. So the daily C dose should probably be split four ways and taken every six hours. Even then blood C levels will shoot up and down four times a day, but the important thing is to get rid of that eighteen-hour vitamin C blind spot. Dividing the dosage still further would smooth things out better; the more spread out the dose the closer, presumably, to nature's intentions—whatever they are.

And did nature intend for the common cold to be so common? It doesn't seem fair somehow that homo sapiens should happen to be the creature that's easily the one most vulnerable to viruses. Over a thousand viral varieties depend exclusively on human hospitality, and new ones are popping up all the time. The situation is so lopsidedly anti-us that one wonders what cosmic crime we might have committed to deserve such a punishment. Is viral vulnerability the price we pay for having left paradise, the jungle of Eden—and vitamin C?

In this department there are suggestions, guesses, profound and elaborate theories, lies, fantasies and out and out hallucinations—all amid a modest sprinkling of facts. All the stuff that's come out about C and the common cold is really interesting, but proof will have to wait until the field gets a little more organized. Until then, however, we can let our imaginations run wild.

Here, for example, are a few facts. (1) Vitamin C is able to react with histamine in such a way as to inactivate it. (2) When rats are making histamine they also lay in a good supply of ascorbate. (3) Vitamin C is famous for being able to keep capillary walls firm and tight, while histamine opens them up. Conclusion (???): Vitamin C is nature's anti-histamine.

All the tempting connections between C and colds have encouraged the idea that C stands for Common Cold Cure. To test the idea, lots and lots of experiments have been done with people; providing us with thousands of successes and thousands of failures. Looking through all these reports can give us a feel for what works and what doesn't, especially what doesn't.

We can pretty safely say, for example, that one great big dose of vitamin C won't help your cold. This makes a kind of sense since the kidneys get rid of it so quickly. It must be that the vitamin's got to be around more or less continuously if it's going to have any effect. So it should be taken at least four times a day. And the amount that should be taken appears to be a minimum of about two-thirds of a gram.

Now for a very common but confusing observation. Once you first notice the symptoms of a cold—any symptoms—you've got about a day to start with the vitamin C or you might as well forget about it. If you use the C either too little or too late, you'll probably have the same cold you'd have had otherwise except that it'll last a few days longer. This feature of vitamin C is a tough one to explain. About the best suggestion so far is that ascorbate might be necessary for making interferon.

When a cell gets invaded by a virus it does everything it can to keep the same thing from happening to his fellow cells. The cell starts making a special kind of protein which it then distributes to its neighbors. This protein makes changes inside the other cells which make them unappetizing to would-be viral invaders. This is the kind of thing that must be done early in the game because the special protein won't help once the virus has penetrated the victim cell. That protein is called interferon.

Just how vitamin C might be involved in making interferon is anybody's guess, but if this shot in the dark is anywhere near the target it will answer a lot of questions. It seems to take a day or so for cold viruses to distribute themselves throughout the body once symptoms have begun to appear. So the idea is to get interferon to the as-yet-unaffected cells soon enough for the interferon to interfere, and nip the infection in the bud. The viruses have actually been in the body for a week or more by that time, slowly spreading, but we don't usually find out about it until symptoms develop.

Some symptoms are caused by the actual damage the viruses do, while others come from the body's protective system, taking special measures to combat the disease. Muscle aches, fatigue, and irritation to the eyes, nose and throat seem to fall into the first category, while fever and congestion belong to the second. If vitamin C can prevent viruses from attacking cells then it's easy to understand how it might relieve cold-induced muscle aches, etc. But what about congestion?

With its delicate mucous membranes under siege from a swarm of vicious viri, the body wants to be super-careful to keep all the other pests from getting into the act. For this purpose we each have our own private army of antibodies and white cells. Actually it's more like a navy, because these guys get where they're going by swimming, and without water they're not going anywhere.

So the body sends histamine to the affected tissues, and histamine apparently causes the cells there to make E-prostaglandins, which in turn open up the capillary flood gates. The tissue swells with water that leaks out of the capillaries and the antibodies and what-have-you can then backstroke on in to keep the peace. Otherwise a serious bacterial infection could develop there. And that's why there's congestion.

Vitamin C might be acting against this simply by virtue of being an anti-histamine, but there are some other intriguing connections. White cells, for instance, are loaded with ascorbate; in fact they serve as the body's principal storage area for the vitamin. White cells kill bacteria and such, basically by swallowing them whole and digesting them. But, just to make sure, the white cells also use a strong poison called hydrogen peroxide. And hydrogen peroxide is nothing more than two hydroxyl groups stuck together like siamese twins. Hydroxyls again.

And then there's aspirin. We know that aspirin, for all its harmful effects, really can reduce some cold symptoms, and we also know how. It does it by preventing the manufacture of those E-prostaglandins. If you take aspirin when you don't have a virus, the white cells will suddenly start absorbing less C than usual. But take it when you have a virus and for some crazy reason they start absorbing more. What does it all mean? Well, if we had a sure answer to that one we could take a thousand scientists off the payroll. But it might mean that the only things aspirin does for a cold would be done just as well by vitamin C. But why should we want to inactivate our body's own defences anyway?

If ascorbate does anything to activate interferon and the interferon gets activated before the virus attack is fully underway, then there's no reason to have congestion because there isn't going to be any disease. But if you wait until the viruses are already firmly entrenched in your system, then activating interferon with vitamin C will come too late to stem the tide and messing up your body's defences will only make the cold that much harder to get rid of. So use the vitamin early and completely, or not at all.

The connections between colds and C are vague; we don't really know why it works. We don't even know if it works, but we'd like to. So if you feel like trying it out on one of your colds, by all means do—there doesn't seem to be any danger. And then spread the word, tell people what happened. That's two-thirds of a gram every six hours. If there has to be a longer stretch between doses (like if you're going to sleep) try increasing the doses in between accordingly, only make sure you're taking vitamin C.

Leave a vitamin C pill sitting around for a few days and it's not vitamin C any more, it's dehydro C, which won't help your cold. Exposure to oxygen, heat and even light all encourage this malign molecular metamorphosis. So keep your bottle tightly sealed, in the dark and, if you can, in your freezer. But even under the best conditions the vitamin will still decompose, so bottles that have been hanging around for many months won't count for much.

If, however, you're not combatting a cold, you can probably live very happily without C supplements—provided your diet contains its share of fresh fruits and salads. Don't, however, confuse fruits with their commercial juices. The Tropicana company sells an orange juice which is pasteurized. They inform us that if it isn't in the orange, it isn't in the juice; but that doesn't mean that if it is in the orange, it *is* in the juice. And one of the more important things that is but isn't is vitamin C. It's unlikely that even a single molecule of this fragile vitamin could withstand the high heat used in pasteurization. But at least there's always frozen orange juice . . . . right?

The problem is copper. You see, copper has this amazing

property, the ability to transform C to dehydro C with one instantaneous touch of its magic wand. And nothing happens to copper in the process so it can do it over and over again, as often as it gets the chance. Put one copper atom into a solution of vitamin C and it will oxidize every ascorbate molecule it contacts. Leave it in there long enough and there mightn't be any vitamin C left. Now consider that tap water usually has a pretty fair amount of copper in it, coming either from the water itself or from copper tubing through which it may flow (especially if you have those bluish-green copper stains in your sink). Copper was once the hottest thing in plumbing.

Dehydro C is not only not good for you, it's bad for you. Doctors interested in diabetes have been eyeing dehydro C for years. Diabetes is insulin insufficiency, and insulin is made in the pancreas. Inside the pancreas are little colonies called the islets of Langerhans, and inside the islets of Langerhans are special cells called beta cells. Inside the beta cells are little granules in which the insulin-making machinery is housed. And dehydro C de-granule-ates the beta cells. Diabetics also have unusually high levels of dehydro C in their blood.

Another reason not to take dehydro C supplements is that dehydro C can destroy chromosomes. In fact it was found that if you mix a large amount of C with a fair amount of copper in a rat's stomach, you'll make him a strong candidate for stomach cancer. There are a lot of differences between rats and people, but there are more similarities than differences.

On the bright side, vitamin C has been reported to lower blood cholesterol somewhat. This one can believe. One of the more important things that can happen to the body's cholesterol is conversion to cholic acid or deoxycholic acid, two key constituents of bile. The reaction that causes that conversion is a hydroxylation reaction.

If a little extra C might be helpful to people with high blood cholesterol, it seems mandatory for those who smoke. The hot fumes can oxidize ascorbate instantly in the lungs, destroying as much as 100 mg. per cigarette. And of course this applies no more to tobacco than to marijuana. But smoke can't destroy what isn't there and the average man has only about a gram and a half, total, in his body. So even the heaviest smoker couldn't lose more than about half a gram a day. But how to replace it?

Eating habits being what they are at present, very few of us get more than a fraction of a gram of ascorbate per day (any gorillas in the audience may turn to the next chapter), so we must either change our eating habits if we want more, or turn to supplements.

The C supplements come as liquids, powders and crystals but mostly they come as pills—all-natural pills, all-synthetic pills, everything in-between, time release pills, little swallowable pills and big delicious chewable candy pills. In making these pills, there's no point in whittling a natural C source down till there's nothing left but C because what you'd get would be identical with the stuff that's synthesized from scratch, only a hundred times more expensive. You can stop a few steps short of complete purity though, and get something that's only twice as expensive as, and maybe even better than, pure vitamin C.

Some of nature's ascorbic acid is found complexed with other things called bioflavonoids. These can slow down the oxidation of our vulnerable vitamin both in the plants that make them and in the bottles that store them. Their value inside our bodies is very debatable, but they're certainly not harmful.

The chewables often contain sugar, saccharin or god-knows-what else, and the FDA doesn't seem too concerned whether they list their non-vitamin ingredients or not. It's about time they were.

A level teaspoon of pure C powder will contain about 4.4 grams.

Also available but rarely seen is sodium ascorbate. A gram of this would contain about 0.1 grams of sodium.

Large amounts of vitamin C in the stomach have been known to cause discomfort and indigestion, in some cases leading to ulcers. One idea would be to take your ascorbate with meals to dilute its acid effect. But how could an organ that loves a strong acid like hydrochloric be bothered by a weak one like ascorbic? It seems more likely that the irritation comes from dehydro C. In that case one should be sure of the freshness of the pill that one takes and if you already have an ulcer, keep a close eye on it. As for meals, it's hard to say—because any meal will have plenty of copper and iron in it, and these magic potions can turn Dr. Jekyll into Mr. Hyde.

In the "Vive la difference!" department we can find some more interesting things about vitamin C. Women seem to absorb more C than men, and store more of it longer. This adds up to women needing only about three-quarters what men need to do the same thing. (The FDA has yet to make this official, but then the FDA has yet to make itself official.) And women don't get scurvy as easily as men. People investigating this datum have suggested the incredible idea that women, with their biochemical backs to the wall, are able to *make* a little vitamin C—not enough to keep them from getting scurvy, just enough to raise some crazy questions.

Maybe, for instance, our blueprints for the enzymes that

make vitamin C weren't really clobbered out of existence by cosmic rays, but were instead just quietly locked away, to be made available only to women and in extreme situations. This could be seen as the first in a series of small steps toward C self-sufficiency for our species. But it might also mean that nature knew what it was doing after all, and had some reason for keeping large C doses out of our systems. Maybe nature knows something that we don't, but should.

Vitamin C (mg/100 gm food)

beans, dairy,		romaine lettuce	18
nuts, grain and meat	0.	raspberries	18
plums	1.9	squash	22
tamarinds	2.0	tomatoes	23
lettuce	2.4	tangerines	23
pomegranates	3.0	loganberries	24
watermelon	3.2	radosjes	24
grapes	3.6	lychees	25
apples	4.0	pitangas	25
pears	4.0	mangoes	27
peaches	6.1	breadfruit	29
casaba melon	7.0	limes	31
carrots	8.0	green onions	32
cherries	8.7	cantaloupe	33
rhubarb	9.0	lemons	35
pumpkin	9.0	dandelion greens	35
persimmons, Jap.	9.0	kumquats	36
mammee fruit	9.0	elderberries	36
apricots	10.	papaya	37
cranberries	10	grapefruit	38
bananas	10	cabbage	47
endive	10	oranges	50
onions	10	spinach	51
cucumbers	11	persimmons, native	52
mulberries	12	strawberries	57
nectarines	13	chives	70
blueberries	14	amaranths	80
sapodillos	14	watercress	80
avocadoes	14	green peppers	110
quinces	15	parsley	170
honeydew melon	15	black currants	200
royal jelly	16	guavas	240
tangelos	16	acerola cherries	1100
pineapple	17	rose hips	3000

Recommended Daily Allowances
for Vitamin C

birth - 1 year	35 mg
1 - 10 years	40
11+	50
pregnant women	60
lactating women	80

Vitamin D

The body makes all its steroid hormones out of cholesterol, and it has evolved some sophisticated ways of doing it. These conversions are done through enzymes—with one exception. The steroid that's made in this exceptional way is able to affect some special membranes in such a way as to let calcium pass through them more easily.

In the small intestine it allows us to absorb more of our food's calcium; in the kidney it permits re-collection of calcium that would otherwise be lost in the urine; and in the bone it persuades reserves in the form of structural calcium to cut loose and become active calcium. And we probably played around with a lot of elaborate ways to make this hormone before we found the shortcut. It turns out that sunlight can do most of the work for us.

The dermis (the skin beneath our skin) and sweat glands both contain liberal amounts of something called dehydro-cholesterol. If a light particle with just the right amount of energy strikes it, the dehydro-cholesterol molecule shakes down to a molecule of vitamin D_3, cholecalciferol (that's calcium somehow stuck into the middle of cholesterol, sort of). The energy that's just right translates to a color down toward the high-energy violet end of the spectrum (wavelength 2800 angstroms). These energetic photons are very easily distracted by air molecules on their way down to us. Sunlight coming from near the horizon passes through much more air than the noonday sunlight (see figure 2). So light from sunrise and sunset isn't of much use for making vitamin D. The same goes for winter light because the winter sun tends to be close to the horizon (that's why winters are cold), with the effect getting worse as you get closer to the poles. But vitamin D isn't the hormone we were talking about.

The dehydro-cholesterol from the sweat glands goes up onto the surface of the skin and gets converted to D, but it's so easily washed away that the D in the dermis is probably much more important to our health. This D is taken back into the bloodstream and shipped to the liver where a hydroxyl is stuck onto it to make hydroxy D, and this is the hormone.

If for some reason this set-up breaks down and the blood calcium falls dangerously low, an alarm rings in four little glands in the neck. These, the parathyroid glands, respond with a special hormone of their own, which travels down to the kidney and activates a special enzyme that adds a second hydroxyl to D, making hydroxy D into dihydroxy D, which is ten times stronger. If even this doesn't give enough calcium, problems start to appear. The organs on which our lives depend, starved for calcium, turn to the bones to get it. And all the while, calcium is needlessly being lost through the kidney. The bones slowly soften and become brittle, brittle enough to fracture almost spontaneously. In adults this condition is called osteomalacia, in children, rickets.

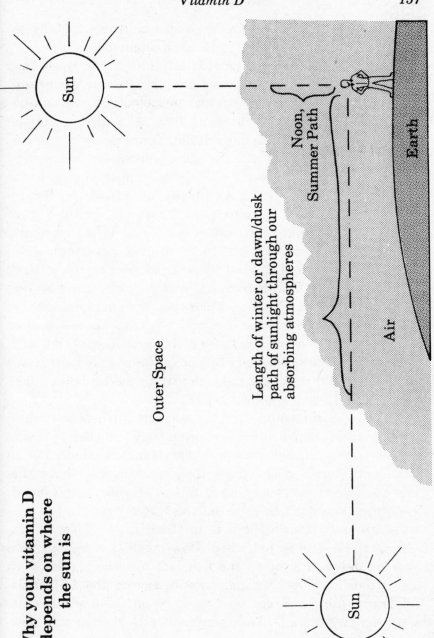

Why your vitamin D depends on where the sun is

Outer Space

Length of winter or dawn/dusk path of sunlight through our absorbing atmospheres

Noon, Summer Path

Sun

Sun

Earth

Air

But the only way to get those conditions these days is to shun the sun and stubbornly refuse D supplements.

When it comes to supplements, vitamin D_2 becomes important. You get D_2 by exposing something called ergosterol to violet light. Ergosterol is found in molds and yeasts, and it differs from dehydro-cholesterol by a methyl group it lacks. D_2 (ergocalciferol) also differs from D_3 by the same methyl, but D_2 and D_3 have the same potency in the body.

To put a once-and-for-all end to the danger of rickets in American children, the government undertook to fortify milk, the key calcium source, with vitamin D. They had found that putting yeast under an ultraviolet lamp, irradiating them, turned all their useless ergosterol into wonderful vitamin D_2. First they tried feeding irradiated yeast to the cow. It worked but it was very expensive so the government didn't like that. Then they tried irradiating the cow. That worked too but the cow probably didn't like it. Now they just remove the D from the irradiated yeast, add it directly to the milk, and everybody's happy. A quart contains about 400 international units (IUs) and an IU is a fortieth of a millionth of a gram of D.

Fish live in a medium that screens out ultra-violet, making it tough for them to make D our way. So they make it the old way, with enzymes and everything. D (that's D_3) is made and stored in the fish's liver, making fish liver the only really concentrated source of the vitamin to be found in nature. You don't have to eat the whole liver though, because all the vitamin there is in there in the form of oil, which can be, and is, extracted. How much D is in your fish liver oil depends a lot on the fish, not just the species, but the actual fish. The average concentration is about 1000 IU per gram of oil, with cod tending to be on the low side of it and tuna on the high. And there's some D, though considerably less, in non-fish livers (people also store their D in the liver) and eggs.

The idea of getting vitamin D by mouth is a new one on nature (unless our ancestors used to lick each other after sunbathing), but why not take advantage of it? After all, it's virtually eliminated the once-major disease of rickets. It's quite absorbable, though we must of course, take the usual precautions for fat-soluble vitamins—having a healthy liver (for bile) and some oils in the diet. But the advent of rich oral sources of D has brought with it a very serious problem of its own, one we never had before. It's as though the vengeful spirit of rickets has returned to haunt us in a new manifestation—hypercalcemia.

A large amount of D in the body means a large amount of hydroxy D too. But hormones like hydroxy D and its big brother, dihydroxy D, have got to be watched very carefully. Each hormone molecule is like a tiny spigot stuck into the membrane on which it acts. With too few spigots too little happens, but with too many, too much happens. The intestines absorb much more calcium, the kidneys excrete less, and a flood of structural calcium pours through the membranes that surround our bones—the blood calcium soars. When the blood level gets high enough, the calcium can't help but start precipitating out of the blood and into wherever it happens to be at the moment. So while the bones slowly dissolve away, the heart, lungs, kidneys and blood vessels are slowly but surely petrified with calcium. It could kill you.

Besides being harmful, large D doses can be very hard to get rid of once they're inside you, so use this vitamin carefully. Dangerous doses range from ten to forty thousand IU per day in adults and three to four thousand in infants. Single doses in the hundreds of thousands can be fatal unless there is a clear case of rickets. Signs of overuse include drop in weight, loss of coordination and numbness or tingling in the extremities. But interpretation of such ambiguous signs should be left to a doctor.

You may be wondering what happened to vitamin D_1. There actually was such a thing but it turned out to be a mixture of D_3 and a related steroid. Ds four through seven also exist, all of them synthetic and all having a potency of about a tenth that of Ds two and three.

On the average you can expect about 1 IU per hour to be made for every square centimeter of skin you expose to the sun. Persons with very dark skin will get about a third as much because their opaque epidermis absorbs much of the light before it can reach the dermis. Dark skin is a feature of areas where there is plenty of sun and people wear little clothing—they can afford less D. We can't do anything about the sun but, come summer, most of us could sacrifice à little clothing.

Artificial lighting won't make the D conversion because it tends toward the reddish colors at the opposite end of the spectrum. Our mind unconsciously adapts to the difference for us, but the unbiased eye of color film shows clearly how much bluer it is outside than in.

If your sunlight comes to you through a cloud you'll get about the same amount of D. But if it comes to you through smog you'll probably get none.

Vitamin D (IU/100 gm)			
eggwhite	0.0	eggs	48
bass	1.0	liver	50
bee pollen	1.6	sunflower seeds	92
cow milk	4.0	shrimp	150
cottage cheese	4.0	mushrooms	150
human milk	6.0	egg yolk	160
corn oil	9.0	tuna	250
oysters	10.	salmon	400
cream	15	sardines	500
cheeses	30	cod liver oil	20,000
butter	40	tuna liver oil	10,000,000

Recommended Daily Allowance
for Vitamin D

birth - 22 years	400 IU
23+	0
pregnant women	400
lactating women	400

Vitamin E

E is a vitamin whose subtle mode of action, though it extends deeply into the biggest health problem this country faces today, has evaded the most powerful probes of technology. So we're left with thousands upon thousands of observations, and scarcely a glimmer of understanding as to why what is happening is happening. Needless to say there's room for a lot of argument, but the evidence seems to suggest that heart disease is what we get for ignoring vitamin E for the past hundred or so years.

Although exactly how is still very much a mystery, it looks as if E acts as a kind of conductor for the body's mass transportation system; preventing dangerous interactions among the passengers. The passengers that have to be watched most closely are the oxidizing agents, the most important of which are oxygen and its free radical relatives. Oxygen has this very strong inclination towards sneaking off with a pair of someone else's hydrogens so it can become H_2O, water.

The kind of molecule most susceptible to this kind of

damage is fat, and the most susceptible fat is the unsaturated fat. A saturated fat is one that has all single bonds between the atoms; an unsaturated fat has some doubles and triples; the more doubles and triples there are, the more unsaturated it is. But each double or triple bond is a chink in the molecule's armor, a place where an obnoxious oxygen can slip in and do its dirty work.

If the outcome of this process were nothing worse than water, nobody'd be complaining. What we get instead are lipid peroxides, the rest of the fat molecule. Peroxides aren't as bad as oxygen. They're worse. They attack membranes with a vengeance, rupturing red cells and vessel walls. And every cell laid to waste in this fashion becomes the source of thousands of additonal free radicals.

Vessels damaged in this vicious cycle start collecting cholesterol and initiate atherosclerosis, but they also collect something else, something called ceroid. Ceroid is an ugly brown gook that results from the fusion of disintegrating remnants of what used to be unsaturated fats. If the unsaturated fats didn't disintegrate there wouldn't be any ceroid. Vitamin E can protect them.

Vitamin E seems to act in a similar way to prevent blood from clotting inside our veins. When blood is exposed to the air, things mix which start the chemical reaction that leads to production of fibrin, the stuff of which clots are made. In the absence of vitamin E those things can mix even without air exposure, resulting in a little gooey glob that travels along smaller and smaller vessels till it hits one its own size. Then it catches, blocks traffic, and deprives the tissue served by that vessel of oxygen. In the coronary arteries that serve the heart this means a heart attack, in the brain a stroke, and in the lungs a pulmonary embolism. But in all cases it means the death of a goodly chunk of tissue through oxygen starvation.

Not that oxygen starvation has to happen in this catastrophic fashion. It can happen gradually, as when atherosclerosis slowly strangles the coronary arteries, bringing on the intense pain of angina pectoris as the dying muscle cells scream for oxygen with their last breath. Or in advanced cases of diabetes, where disintegrating vessels in the arms and legs cause the whole limb to asphyxiate, necessitating amputation.

And even where oxygen lack didn't do the damage, it can greatly compromise the repair job. Following any severe burn, wound or infection, large numbers of cells are left temporarily cut off from the oxygen supply. How many of these stranded cells will survive depends on how much oxygen gets to the area and how fast. If the rescue effort fails, the cells die and are replaced by scar tissue. About the only function that scar tissue serves is to take up space, and as the years pass it contracts on itself, slowly but inexorably.

So what's all this got to do with vitamin E? Only that E can practically double the oxygen available to a given tissue, thereby combatting the damage done by clots, relieving angina, inhibiting diabetic gangrene, and preventing the growth of scar tissue. Scars may not seem like the worst thing in the world. If they're just on the skin they're pretty harmless, but if they're inside you they can be nasty. Internal scars left by the surgeon's scalpel tug painfully and relentlessly at metal stitches, blood vessels, nerves, everything—when they start their gradual shrinkage. A bladder infection can leave scars that decrease the bladder's filling capacity as they contract.

Rheumatic fever introduces millions upon millions of barbaric bacteria to the walls, valves and muscle of the heart. These voracious invaders will chomp away at your ticker for weeks until the fever drives them out. If there is insufficient vitamin E around (as happens about ninety-nine point ten per cent of the time), then the bacteria, as they leave, will leave behind them a badly damaged shell of a heart in which scar tissue abounds. As years pass and E lack persists, the contracting scars begin to pull apart the already weakened structure that supports them—and eventually, even if it takes decades, rheumatic heart disease will kill.

One of the things E does to fight scar tissue is to encourage the proliferation of new vessels into damaged tissue. We know it does it but we don't know how. Maybe it can all be explained in terms of oxygen efficiency. And maybe oxygen efficiency can be explained in terms of all that oxygen that E, as an antioxidant, keeps out of trouble-making reactions—thus saving it for useful uses. And maybe not.

As an antioxidant, vitamin E could be protecting our sex hormones. That might explain why male rats have no sex life without it, but it doesn't explain why male people are as potent with as without it. More fruitful is the idea that E protects the highly oxidation-susceptible sperm cells, thus making semen more fertile.

But something was said earlier about heart disease, something that recalls the fact that E is the one vitamin most abused by the milling process. Milling began in this country in the late 1800s. The first case of death by heart attack was diagnosed here around 1910. In the years since, white bread became a staple food throughout America and heart attack our most popular exit into the next world. Now men of great integrity are telling us that vitamin E can act against all the major forms of heart disease, indeed, cure them. It could be the start of something, and the end of something.

Plants make oils that are very high in polyunsaturates, oils that require plenty of antioxidant protection. To deal with that, the plants developed some antioxidants called tocopherols. There are four of them—alpha-, beta-, gamma-, and delta-tocopherol. And the alpha is E. The others act a little like E but not nearly as much as E itself. The total tocopherol of an oil is proportional to the lightness of its texture, the amount of unsaturates it contains. It also depends on how much bleaching, filtering, heating, refining and deodorizing the oil has suffered. E is an impatient passenger; the more stops the train makes before it gets to you, the less chance that E will be on it.

The FDA, ever anxious to keep boredom from our doors, have given us something new to do with our minds—to remember that an IU is an international unit which is a milligram of synthetic alpha tocopherol acetate, making this an industry-oriented unit. We'll stick to milligrams. Meats and vegetables, even cooked, do have modest amounts of vitamin E in them. With a little luck and a lot of care a body can find itself around 20 mg of E per day in its food and that's usually plenty. The kinds of doses seen in vitamin E therapies do tend to fall between ten and a hundred times this amount, but then they're often trying to undo the effects of a lifetime of deprivation.

But please, do NOT try treating a serious condition by yourself. If your health is important to you, treat it to a doctor. And if you've seen some bad doctors then keep looking, the odds are in your favor. The effect that vitamin E can have on blood pressure is unpredictable. Sometimes it'll increase the heart rate and raise it, other times it'll open up some vessels somewhere and lower it. If you have rheumatic heart disease, too much vitamin E can kill you.

Otherwise, however, vitamin E is quite safe. Upwards of a thousand milligrams a day can be taken without side effects. One reason for this is that the body is really careful about letting the blood E level rise. Changing the dietary E from 100 to 500 mg a day will only raise the blood E 20%. The first benefits of E therapy aren't expected before many days of sustained use and the rest take many weeks.

To get hundreds of milligrams of E from your food you'd have to drink cups and cups of oil every day. Besides the inconvenience and expense of this operation there's the fact that it wouldn't really work anyway, since our ability to absorb fat-solubles is limited by the amount of bile the liver produces. Since we need another way, and making E is easy and profitable, the inevitable has happened.

Synthetic alpha tocopherol is pretty much the same as what's found in nature, there being one small difference. If you were swimming around in a bottle full of exact copies of yourself and suddenly you encountered one face to face, would it be like looking in the mirror? In most ways it would, but suppose you're left-handed. The guy in the mirror is right-handed. Check it out. He's right-handed, and no amount of twisting, turning, or standing on your head can make you into him or him into you.

Natural vitamin E molecules are right-handed, all of them. They're called d-alpha tocopherol, d for *dextro* which is from a Latin word that means right-handed. But synthetic vitamin Es are liable to bump into a mirror-image of themselves, one that's identical but left-handed—because the manufacturing process knows no way to discriminate between the two forms, so you get both in roughly equal proportions. The question is, does *l*-alpha (*l* for *levo*) have any use in our bodies at all? Could it even confuse the body's use of d-alpha? Or can we use them interchangeably?

Until there are answers, most of the E in supplements will be taken from natural sources, 100% d-alpha. Concentrated down from vegetable oil fractions, the vitamin surfaces in tablets, gelatin-coated capsules, shampoos, lotions and skin creams. The creams contain up to 100 mg per gram and are especially good for burns, as is the liquid vitamin. It should be rubbed into the skin for a few minutes—the skin will eat it up.

Alpha Tocopherol Strengths

1 mg of synthetic (d and l)	E acetate	= 1.00 IU
1 mg of synthetic	E	= 1.10 IU
1 mg of natural (d only)	E succinate	= 1.21 IU
1 mg of natural	E acetate	= 1.36 IU
1 mg of natural	E	= 1.49 IU

Vitamin E (mg/100 gm)			
mushrooms,		corn	1.7
skim milk	0.0	barley	1.7
cow milk	0.060	oats	1.7
cottage cheese	0.100	parsley	1.8
lamb	0.20	butter	1.9
pig meat	0.20	broccoli	2.0
beans	0.20	vegetable oils	2.3
cow meat	0.20	asparagus	2.5
medium molasses	0.20	spinach	2.9
chicken	0.20	soy lecithin	4.8
human milk	0.23	cashews	5.1
fruits	0.30	cod liver oil	5.4
vegetables	0.30	peanuts	6.5
turkey	0.30	brazil nuts	6.5
yeasts	0.40	almond oil	7.5
carrots	0.50	cabbage	7.8
shrimp	0.50	mayonnaise	12.0
halibut	0.60	margarine	13.
apples	0.60	olive oil	14.
liver	0.60	almonds	15.
coconut oil	0.60	peanut oil	16.
cream	0.70	soy oil	16.
coconut	1.00	apricot oil	21.
leeks	1.0	hazelnuts	21.
eggs	1.0	corn oil	21.
cheeses	1.0	walnuts	22.
lard	1.0	sesame oil	26.
rye	1.2	wheat	30.
bee pollen	1.3	sunflower seeds	31.
salmon	1.4	safflower nuts	35.
pecans	1.5	cottonseed oil	44.
avocadoes	1.5	wheat germ	160.

Recommended Daily Allowances
for Vitamin E

	men	women
birth - 6 months	4 IU	
6 months - 1 year	5	
1 - 3 years	7	
4 - 6 years	9	
7 - 10 years	10	
11 - 14 years	12	
15+	15	12
pregnant women		15
lactating women		15

Vitamin K

K stands for *koagulate* which is Danish for coagulate, which is English for clot. Without K the blood kan't klot. There are a dozen or so so-called "clotting factors", all different, and you're not going to have a clot without each and every one. K is necessary for the synthesis of factors 7, 9 and 10. Without plenty of it you clot slower, bruise easier and have a tendency toward internal bleeding. But deficiencies are pretty rare.

One reason is that vitamin K is available in food, especially liver and green leaves. Another is that the bacteria in our intestines make lots of it, though we don't know for sure how much of it is absorbed. What's made by the bacteria is vitamin K all right, but it's not the same thing found in leaves. Leaf K is called K_1 (phylloquinone) and bacteria K, K_2 (farnoquinone), with the potencies being roughly the same. K_3 (menadione) is artificial and about twice as strong.

Vitamin K Strengths

1 mg of K_1 = 500 IU
1 mg of K_2 = 400 IU
1 mg of K_3 = 1000 IU

An adult needs an estimated tenth of a milligram per day and an infant about a thousandth. Newborns are routinely supplemented with K by injection because they are too old to get it through the navel as they did in the womb, and too young to have developed the bacterial population that will make it for them. This is especially important because an infant can, in a few days, get a K deficiency that would take weeks in an adult. At the same time though, an excess (say, more than 100 mg) that would give an adult a mild attack of nausea will cause permanent nerve damage in a child, especially a premature one.

But suppose you don't want your blood to clot, or suppose it clots too much and you want to normalize it. Well there are probably a dozen worthwhile approaches to this problem but modern medicine always seems to want to do things the hard way. Rather than help the body help itself, pharmacologists prefer crippling some other body process that was just minding its own business. In this case they decided to block the body's use of vitamin K.

Normally, K shuttles back and forth between two enzymes to get its job done, but modern medical know-how has found a way to keep K away from the second enzyme. In doing so, the anti-coagulant drugs (coumadin, panwarfin, sintrom, miradon, dicumarol, etc.) prevent the liver from making those three clotting factors, at least to some extent. This seems a sad way to proceed when something as safe as vitamin E is available. Meanwhile, the anti-coagulants are causing toxic side effects, hemorrhaging and dangerous interactions with practically every other drug on the market.

You can get the same kind of effect without drugs by simply damaging your liver, the place where the clotting factors are made. You can do it with lead poisoning, alcoholism and most of the anti-natural concoctions that pass for medication these days, from aspirin on up.

Hormones also play a part in this bio-molecular drama. Women are somewhat insulated against the effects of a K deficiency because the female sex hormones that circulate within them just happen to promote clotting. But this, like everything else in life, can also be pushed too far the other way. Too much estrogen can get the blood's clotting tendency to where it doesn't even wait for an opportunity, and clots just for the pure hell of it, inside us. Birth control pills are, beyond some flour and perhaps a sugar coating, nothing but estrogen.

Vitamin K (mg/100 gm)

oranges	0.0011	coffee	0.039
eggs	0.0020	peas	0.044
cauliflower	0.0020	watercress	0.060
bananas	0.0020	bran	0.069
cow milk	0.0029	potatoes	0.080
green beans	0.0044	liver	0.100
corn oil	0.0071	broccoli	0.20
peaches	0.0079	cabbage	0.25
mushrooms	0.0083	cauliflower	0.28
asparagus	0.0100	soybeans	0.30
corn	0.010	spinach	0.33
carrots	0.010	oats	0.49
eggs	0.012	alfalfa	0.52
strawberries	0.013	pig meat	0.95
honey	0.025	soy lecithin	1.2
tomatoes	0.027	brussel sprouts	1.5
wheat germ	0.033	camembert	16.
cow meat	0.035	cheddar	22

Bioflavonoids

This word refers to a collection of chemicals which are strongly associated with citrus fruits, especially the rind. You read about them here because somebody has been dressing them up in the fancy name of vitamin P. The subject is confusing because of the large number of bioflavonoids involved (rutin, hesperidin, citrin, narigen, esculin, etc.) and the small amount of research that's been done. But still it's safe to' say that while they may have some nutritional value, they have next to no nutritional importance.

Many of the bioflavonoids are rich in hydroxyl groups so the suggestion that they can help or even substitute for vitamin C is natural. This may be happening in plants but in people apparently not. There are also claims that these citric species have an anti-coagulant effect. For the moment they remain claims.

Rutin seems to act as a mild stimulant.

Studies on bioflavonoid occurrence in food are rare and not very useful at that.

Essential Fatty Acids

Biochemically speaking, fats are very useful things. And so are acids. So plants got the idea to tuck some of their sun-derived energy away in the form of fatty acids a long, long time ago. Now a fatty acid that holds as much energy as it possibly can is saturated, made up entirely of single bonds between the carbon links in the chain. But as we know, plants are far from being the most energetic of God's creatures so they don't have to completely fill up their energy coffers. That's why their fats are usually unsaturated (olives, avocados and coconuts being among the exceptions), and unsaturated fats are very different from saturated ones.

Single bonds average two carbons and four hydrogens in every bond, while double bonds have the same number of carbons and take up approximately the same amount of space but have only two hydrogens. Triple bonds have no hydrogen at all. So the less saturated a fat is, the more double and triple bonds it has, the more "empty" it is, the less dense. Consequently the most unsaturated fats feel very light, almost ethereal, to the touch.

But with animals it's a different story altogether. They want to make their energy reserves as compact as possible because they have to lug it around with them wherever they go. Animals also have much greater energy requirements, so they fill their energy jars to the brim when they get the chance. As a result, animal fats are saturated, full of hydrogens, or at least a lot closer to it than plant fats. The saturated fats are greasy, heavy and often solid at room temperature—as are lard, butter and bacon fat.

Since this kind of fat fulfills most of the body's fat functions, it's the kind of fat we make most of. We can, for example, make an eighteen-carbon, fully-saturated fatty acid called stearic acid from scratch, simply by stringing acetates (nine of them) together. Once we've got that we can even convert one of the bonds to a double bond with a special process, and that makes stearic into oleic acid. But that process can only work once on a given molecule, so oleic acid is as far as we can go by ourselves.

Oleic acid is fine for energy purposes, but we also need oil to lubricate our skin and hair, and grease doesn't seem like the best thing to do it with. Something lighter is needed, but the body lacks the equipment for making anything lighter, so we turn to our friends the plants. In plants we find linoleic (18 carbons, two double bonds), linolenic (18 carbons, 3 double bonds) and arachidonic (20 carbons, 4 double bonds) acids—the essential fatty acids. Skin oils are comprised almost entirely of these three acids and food is the only way to provide them. If the food you're eating does that insufficiently, your skin will soon lubricate insufficiently, causing eczema—dry, rough, itching, scaling skin. But if that was the worst that could happen, there wouldn't be much to worry about.

Nowadays there's pretty general agreement about how

hormones work. They're the guys that travel from the general to the soldiers in the field relaying some biochemical battle-plan. But those soldiers, being in the heat of the action, often know things that were never dreamt of in the command post. Shouldn't they have some authority too? Well, as it happens, they do.

If a given tissue decides on its own that it ought to be doing the things it would otherwise do only in response to a hormone, it doesn't have to send somebody over to wake up the gland that's in charge of secreting that hormone. Instead, that tissue induces those hormonal changes with something that acts like the hormone but isn't, something the tissue made itself, something a lot stronger than the hormone, something called a prostaglandin. And prostaglandins are made from arachidonic acid.

No arachidonic acid, no prostaglandins. And likewise, without arachidonic you'll have neither prostacyclin nor thromboxane A_2.

So what, beyond being two more words you won't find in Webster's unabridged, are prostacyclin and thromboxane A_2? Well they're two chemicals that travel around in the blood. Thromboxane A_2 wants the blood to clot; in fact it can be the most potent clot-initiator known when it gets a chance to act. But prostacyclin likes things just the way they are, nice and peaceful. And to keep them that way it blocks the action of thromboxane. It takes one prostacyclin molecule to keep a molecule of thromboxane under control, and since the two rivals are usually made in equal amounts, prostacyclin usually gets its way. But what if there's a wound?

When atmospheric oxygen hits our blood it unleashes poisonous lipid peroxides by the swarm. One immediate effect of this is interference with prostacyclin production, while the making of hardier thromboxane continues. Soon, often in seconds, thromboxane dominates the scene and a clot forms. The clot seals off the oxygen influx, the previously-formed peroxides are dealt with, prostacyclin production resumes, the balance restores itself and everything returns to normal. The body's got it all figured out. And to keep peroxides from working their evil ways inside us, it'll always have vitamin E—or at least would like to.

The EFA's are also a key constituent of lecithin. Without them, we can't make our own lecithin and when our lecithin is decreased, cholesterol starts to bubble out of the blood and into our arteries.

All this notwithstanding, the food industry has never been exactly crazy about polyunsaturates. They talk and talk about how wonderful those fats are, then remove as many as possible in order to improve the shelf life of their product. What they don't remove they complex with commercial anti-oxidants in such a way as to protect them both from rancidity in the bottle and absorption in our stomachs. And then there's hydrogenation.

Hydrogenation is simply saturating the unsaturated fats, filling them up with hydrogens. It's done to give that thick spread-ability to things like margarine and peanut butter. (Some of the things we sacrifice our health for. . . .) And of course every additional hydrogen means more energy value in the fat. If you're starving, then things like that are important but if you're not, it's just that much more exercise you need to burn up the fat you're storing.

At any rate, if you're looking for polyunsaturates in processed food, you're looking in the wrong place, no matter what it says on the label. Lecithin and fresh, cold-pressed vegetable oils are the most concentrated sources, but un- or lightly-cooked plant foods are more than adequate. So are fish. If fishes stored energy as saturated fat they'd all stiffen up like boards as soon as the water got cool.

So they don't.

Oleic acid is not one of the essential ones, but, since our bodies seem capable of converting it to essential linoleic, it seems like one worth knowing about.

Studies on arachidonic acid are just beginning. For a long time it was assumed that plants didn't have any, so nobody bothered to measure it.

Oleic Acid (mg/100 gm)

lima beans	45	lamb	7100
fruits	100	avocadoes	7400
spinach	120	olives	7600
beans	120	coconut oil	8600
barley	200	pig meat	9000
wheat	210	cheeses	9500
rye	280	sesame seeds	10000
corn	340	sunflower oil	12000
rice	660	wheat germ oil	15000
millet	670	cow meat	18000
human milk	1100	safflower oil	20000
cow's milk	1200	walnuts	21000
tuna	1200	sesame oil	21000
chicken	1200	brazil nuts	21000
egg yolk	1200	peanuts	26000
cream	1300	butter	27000
wheat germ	1500	soy oil	27000
spices	1800	cottonseed oil	30000
oats	2200	cashews	34000
turkey	2600	corn oil	35000
coconut	3100	almonds	37000
haddock	3500	cocoa butter	38000
salmon	4200	pecans	44000
veal	4700	lard	46000
soybeans	4900	hazelnuts	50000
flax seeds	5100	peanut oil	54000
eggs	6000	almond oil	69000
sunflower seeds	6000	olive oil	75000

Linoleic acid (mg/100 gm)			
haddock	2.2	coconut oil	2000
sole	7.9	egg yolk	2100
fruits	20	cocoa butter	2100
yogurt	49	olives	2200
venison	120	spices	2400
cream	130	oats	2600
cow milk	140	butter	2700
goat's milk	200	cashews	3200
spinach	200	wheat germ	4400
lima beans	220	linseed oil	8000
salmon	230	hazelnuts	9300
cow meat	240	olive oil	10000
human milk	270	lard	10000
veal	290	almonds	11000
herring	390	peanuts	12000
beans	450	pecans	14000
corn	520	sesame seeds	20000
barley	620	margarine	22000
rice	660	brazil nuts	23000
eggs	780	peanut oil	25000
cheeses	850	walnuts	29000
lamb	1000	sunflower seeds	30000
rye	1200	cottonseed oil	35000
tuna	1200	sesame oil	42000
chicken	1200	wheat germ oil	44000
wheat	1200	walnut oil	48000
turkey	1300	soy oil	52000
soybeans	1400	corn oil	54000
liver	1500	sunflower oil	60000
avocadoes	1900	safflower oil	77000
pig meat	2000		

Linolenic acid (mg/100 gm)			
cod	2.8	sablefish	200
tomatoes	2.8	herring	310
barley	5.5	smelt	370
clams	14.	beans	750
rice	17	pecans	920
tuna	21	egg yolk	930
oysters	30	trout	1000
milk	40	safflower oil	1000
wheat	51	soybeans	1300
rye	60	walnuts	3600
corn	68	cottonseed oil	4100
spinach	80	walnut oil	6000
cow meat	95	spices	7100
lima beans	100	soy oil	7200
sardines	140	sesame seeds	32000
millet	160	linseed oil	52000
sole	160	sesame oil	67000
lamb	190		

Arachidonic acid (mg/100 gm)			
haddock	1.6	swordfish	180
cod	9.6	sardines	280
algae	13	herring	310
human milk	30	sole	320
cow meat	38	mackerel	470
scallops	81	whitefish	480
mussels	90	walnuts	960
tuna	94	walnut oil	1600
lamb	95		

In the case of plants, by the way, these values can vary a lot, depending on where it was grown. Cooler climates tend to shift the oil composition up towards the less saturated fatty acids. Warmer climates mean more saturation.

The Minerals

The vitamins, all of them, are pretty complicated things. Chop up a riboflavin molecule, for example, and you'll find it was made out of four nitrogen atoms, six oxygens, twenty hydrogens and seventeen carbons. But break down, say, a magnesium molecule and all you get is . . . one atom of magnesium. Whereas the vitamins are molecules, the minerals are atoms; elements as opposed to compounds.

And while molecules are forever reacting with one another to make new molecules, nothing short of a nuclear reactor can change an atom. So the minerals don't (they can't) participate directly in the essential interactions of life, though they're no less important for that.

The body depends completely on minerals for its skeleton, the structure that makes the difference between a person and a jellyfish. Some enzymes have also incorporated minerals into their design. But mostly enzymes depend on minerals as an environment in which to operate. In ionized form, dissolved in water, thousands of atoms of a certain mineral surround the enzyme and have a profound effect on the enzyme's workings. Under the influence of one mineral the machine might work just fine, but if the mineral is replaced, even with a very similar one, the enzyme can shut down completely. The body takes good advantage of this feature, using it as an on-off switch.

To do things like this, minerals must be water-soluble—and it turns out that all of them are. And this of course makes them prone to urinary losses via diuresis, and dinner table losses via discarded cooking water. One thing we needn't worry about is loss due to heat, storage, etc.—it's pretty hard to hurt an atom. But you can remove one.

Mineral losses in refined flour vary from mineral to mineral but average about 75%, with similar figures applying for the refining of other grains. The idea of throwing away food is silly anyway, but why throw away the best part?

Animal products have pretty consistent mineral contents because the animals they used to be were very careful not to get either too much or too little; our body is the same way. But plants are a lot more casual about all this. Like animals, plants do need vitamins to live. If, for some reason, the plant is unable to make enough of them, it'll die and never get harvested. So the chances of finding a vitamin-poor plant in your salad are pretty slim. But in most cases, the plant's need for a given mineral is not that strong. So if the mineral happens to be in the soil, the plant will absorb it; and if not, well that's the way it goes. In other words, how much mineral is in the plant depends on how much is in the soil beneath it, and soil compositions vary ridiculously from one place to another. This means that in order to predict how much, say, selenium is in a plant, you'd have to know, maybe to within a square mile, just where it was grown. So all we can do is average.

The idea of things like zinc, copper and iron being in our

food suggests that maybe eating rocks and nails would be a good idea. There are often differences, however, between the organic minerals found in life and the inorganics found in dirt. Living things tend to combine their minerals with enzymes and such when using them, and when they die and become lunch, their minerals remain locked up in this form. It doesn't make it any harder for us to absorb them though, in fact our stomachs expect their minerals to come that way. One especially intimate kind of binding is called chelation, and chelated minerals are very common in food. Chelation keeps minerals from interacting dangerously with other things they might bump into in our abdominal mixmaster (which is otherwise very much a possibility) and speeds mineral absorption. Absorption also requires that the mineral be in solution, and with metals that means that some kind of acid should be on hand to keep it dissolved— another good reason why our stomachs secrete hydrochloric.

We know that vitamins get their unique properties through the structure they have and how many of which atoms went into it. But what is it that makes atoms (and therefore minerals) different?

Well just as molecules are made of atoms, atoms are made of particles. And there are lots of particles—muons, pions, positrons, neutrinos, anti-neutrinos, mesons and dozens of others. All particles are interesting but there are basically only two that make the difference between oxygen and aluminum, and they're the protons and the electrons, with a few neutrons thrown in for weight.

The protons are all huddled together in the center of the atom while the electrons whip around them with extraordinary speed. Electrons arrange themselves in "shells" around the protons and each shell is a very select club. Every electron wants to be a member but there's a problem: a shell can only hold a certain exact number of members. After it fills up the leftover electrons try and make their own club. Maybe they'll have enough people to do it and maybe they won't, but when all is said and done there are almost always a few lonely leftovers hanging around on the outside.

Of course these stragglers aren't terribly happy where they are and they take off at the first opportunity. The only thing that keeps them there is their partnership with particles of the opposite electrical gender, the protons. You see, for every electron in an atom, there's a proton; and protons and electrons have a great attraction for one another. An attraction great enough to hold the community together through some pretty rough times. But those left-out outer electrons are still pretty unhappy and itching to do something about it. Dissolving the atom in water gives them their opportunity.

Once in water, the leftover electrons are able to leave the atom and join somebody else's club. In doing so they leave behind them some lonely protons, protons that will always be looking to replace the missing electrons. How much electron-desire the ion (an atom is an ion if it has more protons than electrons or vice versa) has is going to depend on how many electrons are missing. The number of missing electrons is the valence number of the atom. A second factor is how physically close the electrons were to the protons; the closer they were, the more they'll be missed. If you know those two things about an atom and throw in the atom's weight, you know as much about it as your body does.

The Elements

Element	Chemical Symbol	Valence	% (by weight) of human body
Hydrogen	H	1	10
Oxygen	O	-2	65
Carbon	C	4	10
Nitrogen	N	-3	3.
Sodium	Na	+1	0.15
Calcium	Ca	+2	2.
Phosphorus	P	-3	1.1
Sulfur	S	-2	0.25
Potassium	K	+1	0.35
Chlorine	Cl	-1	0.15
Magnesium	Mg	+2	0.05
Iron	Fe	+3	0.004
Copper	Cu	+1	0.00015
Manganese	Mn	+2	0.00013
Zinc	Zn	+2	0.0026
Molybdenum	Mo	+1	0.00037
Iodine	I	-1	0.000040
Vanadium	V	+2	0.000022
Chromium	Cr	+2	0.0000072
Selenium	Se	-2	?

Also present, but probably inactive, are fluorine, nickel, bromine, cobalt (except inside B_{12}), strontium, arsenic, boron, tin and silicon.

Well that's the way the differences and similarities among minerals stack up on an abstract plane. But one luckily needn't know the intimate details of sub-atomic particle physics to lead a healthy, happy life—or we'd all be in trouble.

Iron

Iron is at the very core of the structure of hemoglobin, which is perhaps the body's most important protein. Red cells are what make the blood red, but hemoglobin is what makes the red cells red. In fact hemoglobin is the molecule that actually carries the oxygen from the lungs to every other part of the body, but without iron it can't do it.

One of the body parts that most needs oxygen is muscle, so muscle has its own little protein, myoglobin, for storing the oxygen that hemoglobin brings it. Myoglobin also contains iron. So do cytochromes, which comprise the better part of the electron transport chain. So does catalase, the enzyme that breaks down hydrogen peroxide inside the body; and so do a few other important proteins.

But hemoglobin is far and away the most important, over half the body's iron being tied up in it. If dietary iron is inadequate, hemoglobin is the first to suffer. The result is decreased oxygen transport to the brain and muscles, causing round-the-clock fatigue, headaches, and shortness of breath as the lungs try to compensate. This condition, iron-

deficiency anemia, is associated with the high iron requirements of growing muscles and the high iron losses of pregnancy, breast-feeding and menstruation. The last two cost
about a milligram of iron per day.

Making up a lost milligram in food means eating a lot
more than a milligram. To replace it with animal foods you
need about five milligrams' worth and with plant foods,
about ten; because most eaten iron ain't absorbed. If food
iron doesn't seem like enough, you may turn to supplements. But watch out: with iron as with no other mineral,
it's crucial that your source be chelated (kell' ated). Free
iron, running around loose, can damage all the fat-soluble
vitamins—A, D, E and K—and vitamin C as well. This is
especially true in the case of ferrous sulfate, which is actually dangerous, but also applies to ferric chloride. The
fumarate and gluconate salts, being less likely to dissociate
from their iron, are better choices.

The undeniable importance of iron has persuaded the
FDA to enforce iron enrichment of refined flour, to the extent that twenty-five slices of bread will fulfill the RDA of
an adult. But the importance of many other minerals is just
as undeniable, and so the FDA's failure to act on their be-
half only points up the FDA's own lack of confidence in the
"enrichment" concept. The food industry and FDA alike
would be mighty embarrassed to see twenty-five missing
nutrients being added to all wheat products. But then you'd
think six was embarrassing enough.

Iron (mg/100 gm)

butter, cream	0.00	pig meat	2.9
sea water	0.0010	spinach	3.1
sea salt	0.016	buckwheat	3.1
oranges	0.028	cow meat	3.1
cow's milk	0.041	veal	3.2
human milk	0.050	brazil nuts	3.4
water	0.067	wheat	3.5
coffee	0.087	snails	3.5
plums	0.19	rye	3.7
eggwhite	0.20	cashews	3.8
grapefruit	0.21	clams	4.1
watermelon	0.23	oats	4.5
cabbage	0.38	almonds	4.7
wine	0.39	parsley	5.0
fruits	0.40	oysters	5.6
mushrooms	0.49	mussels	5.8
avocado	0.58	walnuts	6.0
honey	0.75	medium molasses	6.0
halibut	0.80	lentils	6.7
cheeses	0.80	millet	6.8
vegetables	1.00	chickpeas	6.9
berries	1.0	sunflower seeds	7.1
potatoes	1.1	mature sprouts	7.2
maple syrup	1.2	egg yolk	7.2
sprouts	1.2	pistachios	7.2
tuna	1.3	liver	8.8
salmon	1.4	blackstrap molasses	9.1
rice	1.6	wheat germ	9.4
bee pollen	1.6	sesame seeds	10.
coconut	1.7	pumpkin seeds	11
peas	1.7	caviar	12
chicken	1.8	soy lecithin	12
turkey	2.1	kidney	13
corn	2.1	brewer's yeast	17
peanuts	2.1	torula yeast	18
eggs	2.2	bone meal	82
pecans	2.4	seaweeds	90
beans	2.7	kelp	370
barley	2.7	soil	3800

We absorb about 6% of what's eaten.

Recommended Daily Allowances
for Iron

	men	women
birth - 6 months	10 mg	
6 months - 3 years	15	
4 - 10 years	10	
11 - 18 years	18	
19 - 50	10	18
51+	10	10
pregnant women		18
lactating women		18

Calcium and Phosphorus

Our bones are basically calcium phosphate, containing about 40% calcium by weight—along with 45% phosphate, 13% hydroxyl groups, 1% magnesium and smaller amounts of sodium, strontium, citrate, and carbonate. Of these probably only the calcium, phosphate, and hydroxyls are really doing anything to support our bodies, the rest just being along for the ride.

The importance of calcium is driven home by the fact that, unique among the minerals, calcium has its comings and goings hormone-regulated. And there isn't only one hormone involved; besides hydroxylated vitamin D, there's also parathyroid hormone and thyrocalcitonin. The first is for making blood calcium out of bone calcium when the blood calcium gets too low, and the second for reversing the process when it gets too high.

Estrogens, whose structures closely resemble that of hydroxylated vitamin D, have a similar effect. This can be of practical significance to women because the ovaries, which make estrogens, fluctuate in their activity. They're at their weakest throughout puberty and during the time that starts around ten days before menstruation; and they function not at all after menopause. Unless vitamin D and calcium are maintained during these troubled times, a woman leaves herself open to invasion by the symptoms of calcium deficiency. These include irritability, hot flashes, muscle cramping, and finally convulsions. Avoiding these ought to be a simple matter of ingesting more calcium.

If only it were that simple. . . .

First, there's the problem of phosphorus. Phosphorus, which is almost always in phosphate form, is very necessary stuff. If you got a deficiency of it you'd be in real trouble, but that's okay because phosphates are like clothes-hangers, there are always plenty of them around. In fact we usually get lots more than we need. So what's the problem? We'll just use what we need and unload the rest.

The problem is that phosphate is unloaded in the form of calcium phosphate, which means that calcium is lost with each leftover phosphate excreted, whether or not there's leftover calcium to be tossed away like that. So one must ensure that one's food has something like the proper calcium/phosphorus ratio, suggested to be about three calciums for every two phosphori. So watch that.

The other problem is strontium. It's not strontium itself exactly; strontium is calcium's lookalike and it just happens to get confused with calcium sometimes and absorbed by the body. Now mind, strontium doesn't do any harm, it can't replace the functions of calcium but nobody minds if strontium just stands around and watches. The real problem is strontium's ugly relative, strontium-90.

Strontium-90 is a radioactive by-product of nuclear reactions, explosive or otherwise. But it's the explosions that really hurt because they blow the stuff up into the clouds and the clouds travel over to some other part of the world and rain. The rain-water is absorbed by grass and the grass is eaten by cows. The cow's mammary glands take a quick look at the strontium-90, say "Oh boy, calcium!" and soup up the milk with it. Then we drink the milk, absorbing its radioactive rider, which then circulates in the bloodstream for a while. Next, our bones take a quick look at the strontium-90, say "Oh boy, calcium!" and stash it away. The strontium-90, safely and permanently lodged in the bone, commences to radiate a deadly aura of destruction in every direction. Damaging DNA, this radiation can make malignant bone tumors out of normal bone cells and leukemia of the cells in the bone's marrow. Strontium-90 is widely believed to be the principal cause of leukemia.

We can protect ourselves from this insidious menace by getting plenty of calcium, thus making best use of our body's small ability to discriminate between calcium and strontium. We're more likely to admit a substitute if there's too little of the real thing. One calcium source that probably won't help though is bone meal from animals, which also has strontium-90 in it. Fishbone meal is not ideal but it is better; since fish don't eat much grass. A more elaborate idea is eating brown seaweed. Brown seaweed contains alginate, a substance that will bind all the strontium, and only the strontium, in your intestines—making all the strontiums unabsorbable.

But calcium is a nice thing to have if you can find a safe way to get it. Calcium acts as a general stimulant, being the agent responsible for turning on the nerves connecting our senses with the brain, and elsewhere. It also encourages muscles to contract. And contraction is what gives our bodies motion, life.

Calcium (mg/100 gm)

water	0.15	eggs	54
watermelon	3.2	peanuts	69
coffee	3.9	peas	70
plums	4.4	wheat germ	72
honey	4.7	pecans	73
beer	5.0	endive	81
apples	5.3	spinach	93
bananas	5.7	oysters	94
mushrooms	6.1	walnuts	99
whisky	8.0	chard	100
tuna	8.3	cream	100
wine	8.8	maple syrup	100
eggwhite	9.0	buckwheat	110
pig meat	10.	cow's milk	120
fruits	10	sunflower seeds	120
avocadoes	10	kale	130
lamb	11	lentils	130
liver	11	pistachios	130
cow meat	12	beans	130
tomatoes	12	egg yolk	130
chicken	12	greens	150
coconut	13	chickpeas	150
potatoes	14	salmon	150
cantaloupe	14	watercress	150
cucumber	16	brazil nuts	190
millet	20	parsley	200
butter	20	torula yeast	220
flounder	22	almonds	230
corn	22	soybeans	230
turkey	23	caviar	280
oranges	30	medium molasses	290
vegetables	30	carob	350
rice	32	sardines	350
blackberries	32	brewer's yeast	420
human milk	33	sea salt	670
barley	34	cheeses	700
sprouts	35	kelp	1100
wheat	36	sesame seeds	1200
cashews	38	soil	1400
rye	38	seaweeds	1900
sea water	40	dolomite	21000
cabbage	49	bone meal	40000
oats	53		

Most is absorbed.

Recommended Daily Allowances
for Calcium

	men	women
birth - 6 months	360 mg	360 mg
6 months - 1 year	540	800
1 - 10 years	800	800
11 - 14 years	1200	1200
15+	800	800
pregnant women		1200
lactating women		1200

Phosphorus (mg/100 gm)

water	0.0005	pig meat	230
sea water	0.0070	veal	230
sea salt	0.11	halibut	250
bee pollen	0.40	corn	270
honey	3.1	buckwheat	280
coffee	4.0	pecans	290
plums	6.2	chicken	290
maple syrup	8.0	barley	290
apples	10.	millet	310
whisky	10	turkey	320
wine	10	chickpeas	330
human milk	14	kelp	340
eggwhite	16	flounder	340
butter	16	mature sprouts	340
cucumber	18	tuna	350
tea	19	scallops	360
fruits	20	cashews	370
lettuce	22	wheat	380
tomatoes	27	lentils	380
beer	30	rye	380
light molasses	36	salmon	400
vegetables	40	peas	400
avocadoes	42	beans	400
soil	65	peanuts	400
mushrooms	68	oats	410
medium molasses	69	liver	480
sprouts	70	almonds	500
cream	80	soybeans	550
carob	80	walnuts	570
blackstrap molasses	85	egg yolk	570
cow's milk	93	sardines	580
coconut	95	piñon nuts	600
radishes	100	sesame seeds	620
parsley	100	brazil nuts	690
kale	110	sunflower seeds	840
oysters	120	wheat germ	1100
cow meat	190	pumpkin seeds	1100
eggs	200	torula yeast	1500
seaweeds	210	brewer's yeast	1800
lamb	210	soy lecithin	3300
rice	220	dolomite	26000

Most is absorbed.

Recommended Daily Allowances
for Phosphorus

birth - 6 months	240 mg
6 months - 1 year	400
1 - 10 years	800
11 - 14 years	1200
15+	800
pregnant women	1200
lactating women	1200

Magnesium

Magnesium is an enzyme activator. It has the job of turning on most of the enzymes that use B_1, B_2 and B_6 as co-enzymes—that's over a hundred already and there are plenty of others. Since those enzymes need magnesium as badly as they do their co-enzymes, a magnesium deficiency will have symptoms in common with deficiencies of the three vitamins, most notably the convulsions associated with B_6 deficiency.

Another explanation for the convulsions of magnesium deficiency is that magnesium has an effect on muscles opposite to that of calcium—it acts as a muscle relaxer. Calcium allows the muscle to contract when the brain so orders, and magnesium allows it to stretch out again when the job is done. If there's insufficient magnesium the muscles twitch and tremor, and if it gets bad enough you've got spasms registering on the Richter scale.

Calcium and magnesium also interact in another way. A lot of nutrients have their own special transportation in the blood, even some minerals. Iron is carried by a protein

called transferrin and copper by another called ceruloplas-
min. But calcium and magnesium apparently don't rate that
kind of attention—they have to share the services of a protein called albumen. Now see what happens if you suddenly
gobble up a whole lot of, say, calcium. The calcium will be
absorbed and start competing with what magnesium there
is for albumen-space. Odds are that magnesium won't have
much of a chance in such a lop-sided battle. The result is
that magnesium is left at the station without transportation, so it just passes through to fecal excretion. The reverse
could also happen.

But what if you're eating too little of, say, calcium? In
that event the muscles' delicate balance between calcium
and magnesium starts to tip toward magnesium. The muscles might try to compensate by dumping some of the excess. The worse the calcium deficiency gets, the more magnesium they'd dump. So, taking the hint, we can try to balance our intakes of these two minerals accordingly.

The proportion that seems best puts magnesium at about
half the amount of calcium you get. One convenient supplement supplies both minerals. It's called dolomite and it is
calcium magnesium carbonate. Its composition indicates it
should have a magnesium content of around 60% that of the
calcium content (by weight) and it often does, but it sometimes creeps up toward 90%. Why is anyone's guess.

Magnesium (mg/100 gm)

bee pollen	0.24	potatoes	27
water	0.41	tuna	29
vegetable oils	0.70	cheeses	30
butter	2.0	bananas	31
human milk	3.0	avocadoes	37
coffee	5.0	corn	38
apples	5.0	salmon	40
honey	5.5	coconut	44
tea	8.0	barley	55
wine	8.0	spinach	57
pineapple	8.0	chard	65
grapefruit	9.0	mushrooms	68
cream	10.	medium molasses	81
eggwhite	10	rice	120
beer	10	sea water	130
oranges	11	walnuts	130
lettuce	11	oats	140
eggs	12	pecans	140
cow's milk	13	hazelnuts	150
tomatoes	13	soy lecithin	160
fruits	15	pistachios	160
cabbage	15	bone meal	170
egg yolk	16	seaweeds	210
oysters	17	brazil nuts	220
carrots	18	soybeans	240
chicken	19	snails	250
lamb	22	almonds	270
liver	22	wheat germ	320
cow meat	23	sunflower seeds	350
pig meat	23	blackstrap molasses	410
halibut	23	soil	500
vegetables	25	kelp	740
turkey	25	sea salt	2100
cashews	27	dolomite	13000

About 50% is absorbed.

Recommended Daily Allowances
for Magnesium

	men	women
birth - 6 months	60 mg	
6 months - 1 year	70	
1 - 3 years	150	
4 - 6 years	200	
7 - 10 years	250	
11 - 14 years	350	300
15 - 18	400	300
19+	350	300
pregnant women		450
lactating women		450

Potassium and Sodium

Potassium completes the muscle minerals. It acts like magnesium but is much more active in promoting relaxation. Likewise, the effects of potassium deficiency make more sense. . . . well actually none of them make much sense. Why, for instance, should calcium (contractions) deficiency cause convulsions, the ultimate in contractions? Maybe the calcium deficiency causes such magnesium losses that the muscle can't relax anymore. Similarly, why should potassium (relaxation) deficiency cause extreme fatigue, the ultimate in relaxation? Maybe the muscle, unable to relax, contracts itself into a state of total exhaustion. And maybe it all makes sense after all.

Theoretically, a potassium deficiency can only occur through a really severe bout of vomiting or diarrhea because, theoretically, the kidney can tightly control potassium excretion so that none is lost if none is coming in; that way you could never get a deficiency. So much for theory.

One thing that encourages potassium deficiency is sodium excess. Sodium is an element that functions almost entirely outside cells. The cells use an intricate sodium-driven pump to constantly expel water. If there were no sodium outside them, the cells would just swell with water till they burst. The same thing happens in the kidney, but on a larger scale. If the body wants to conserve water, it directs the adrenal cortex to do its stuff. All the cortical steroids have, to greater or lesser extents, the same effect on the kidney: they cause it to retain sodium. The sodium then activates kidney pumps that steer urine-bound H_2O back into the bloodstream. That's why salt (sodium chloride) encourages high blood pressure; it increases the blood's volume.

Yes, sodium is valuable stuff; no homo sapiens should be without one, but there's scarcely any danger of sodium deficiency in this country. It's estimated that daily sodium intake should equal potassium intake should equal about a gram. An average American may or may not get a gram of potassium per day but, thanks to the presence of salt in practically everything, he certainly gets his sodium—about five grans (a teaspoon) of it.

The problem is that sodium, having a stronger electromagnetic pull than potassium, tends to nudge the weaker one out. That's how a perennial excess of sodium could slowly grind a cell's potassium content down to deficiency. As sodium enters the cell to replace potassium it brings water in with it, causing swelling (or edema or dropsy) in the affected tissue. The first muscles to feel the effects are the abdominal ones, and they show it as constipation and proneness to gas and obstruction.

But potassium is also an enzyme activator, there being many enzymes that are activated by potassium and inhibited by sodium. The kind of enzymes involved, those found in the citric acid cycle and electron transport chain, are a kind that are almost completely inactive in cancer cells.

This forms the basis for the idea, suggested by Max Gerson many many years ago, that cancer is the direct result of sodium entering the cells and shutting down their oxidative machinery. The cells are then forced to switchover to fermentation if they are to survive and, *voila*, cancer. Scary thoughts like these are not comforted by the American preference for high-sodium animal products over high-potassium vegetables.

One is tempted to compare our eating habits with our carnivorous economic system.

Potassium (mg/100 gm)

water	0.23	sprouts	320
whisky	2.0	oats	350
yogurt	20.	bananas	370
butter	23	cow meat	370
beer	25	liver	380
tea	25	wheat	390
peaches	27	potatoes	410
coffee	36	chicken	430
sea water	38	millet	430
human milk	50	turkey	440
honey	51	buckwheat	450
plums	63	cashews	460
watermelon	65	walnuts	460
oysters	70	rye	470
concord grapes	78	salmon	510
cheeses	80	halibut	530
wine	80	veal	580
pears	100	lentils	590
grapefruit	110	avocadoes	600
apples	110	pecans	600
cream	110	soil	630
egg yolk	120	peanuts	670
eggs	130	brazil nuts	720
onions	140	sesame seeds	720
cow's milk	140	almonds	770
green grapes	150	chickpeas	800
berries	150	sunflower seeds	920
eggwhite	150	wheat germ	950
cucumber	160	pistachios	980
oranges	170	mature sprouts	1000
maple syrup	180	sea salt	1000
tuna	180	peas	1000
fruits	200	parsley	1000
rice	210	medium molasses	1100
cabbage	230	beans	1200
cantaloupe	250	blackstrap molasses	1700
coconut	260	soybeans	1700
corn	280	brewer's yeast	1900
pig meat	290	torula yeast	2000
lamb	300	seaweeds	5200
vegetables	300	kelp	12000

About 90% is absorbed.

Sodium (mg/100 gm)

salt	39000	cabbage	20
sea salt	30000	human milk	17
kelp	4000	light molasses	15
seaweeds	3300	torula yeast	15
sea water	1900	cashews	15
soil	1400	vegetables	10
eggwhite	190	maple syrup	10
brewer's yeast	120	rice	9.0
eggs	120	beer	7.0
shellfish	100	beans	7.0
oysters	94	unsalted butter	7.0
blackstrap molasses	91	walnuts	6.0
veal	82	wine	5.0
flounder	78	barley	5.0
celery	75	honey	5.0
sablefish	73	soybeans	5.0
spinach	71	peanuts	5.0
lamb	70	potatoes	4.2
liver	70	almonds	4.0
turkey	62	avocadoes	4.0
cow meat	60	scallions	4.0
sesame seeds	60	tomatoes	3.0
pig meat	57	wheat	2.3
egg yolk	53	oats	1.4
fishes	50	clams	1.2
carrots	50	sprouts	1.2
watercress	50	fruits	1.0
yogurt	47	brazil nuts	1.0
cow's milk	47	whisky	1.0
salmon	45	rye	1.0
cream	43	buckwheat	0.91
medium molasses	37	coffee	0.90
tuna	37	corn	0.80
peas	35	water	0.63
sunflower seeds	30	tea	0.43
lentils	30	pecans	0.29
chickpeas	26	watermelon	0.22
parsley	25	millet	0.20
coconut	23		

Most is absorbed.

Manganese

This mineral can sometimes substitute for magnesium in activating B_1 enzymes and is also required by an important biotin enzyme. The enzymes that need manganese are generally involved in carbohydrate metabolism.

Manganese deficiency can halt the making of mucous (which is 100% carbohydrate) and impair the senses of vision, hearing and smell. It also decreases tolerance for glucose (a carbohydrate)—a giant step towards diabetes. The pancreas is very rich in manganese.

It's all very vague but interesting, though not enough so to interest the FDA. We seem to need at least five milligrams per day.

Manganese (mg/100 gm)

sea water	0.0002	bone meal	0.50
water	0.0012	kale	0.50
sea salt	0.0032	yams	0.52
cow meat	0.0050	brewer's yeast	0.53
leeks	0.0100	berries	0.55
cow's milk	0.019	carrots	0.60
chicken	0.020	bananas	0.64
watermelon	0.020	tea	0.69
oranges	0.025	lettuce	0.80
turkey	0.030	grapefruit	0.80
veal	0.030	spinach	0.82
lemons	0.040	parsley	0.94
cantaloupe	0.040	pineapple	1.1
butter	0.040	coconut	1.3
eggwhite	0.043	honey	1.4
eggs	0.053	peanuts	1.5
strawberries	0.060	snails	1.6
pig meat	0.060	rice	1.7
pears	0.060	walnuts	1.8
apples	0.070	turnip greens	1.8
mushrooms	0.080	almonds	1.9
grapes	0.083	beans	2.0
egg yolk	0.088	peas	2.0
lard	0.098	watercress	2.0
fruits	0.100	ginseng	2.0
eggplant	0.11	coffee beans	2.1
kelp	0.15	sunflower seeds	2.5
cucumbers	0.15	brazil nuts	2.8
celery	0.16	barley	3.2
potatoes	0.17	pecans	3.5
cauliflower	0.17	wheat	3.6
vegetable oils	0.18	chestnuts	3.7
tomatoes	0.19	hazelnuts	4.2
apricots	0.20	oats	4.9
fishes	0.20	buckwheat	5.1
liver	0.28	bay leaves	6.7
raspberries	0.28	ginger	8.7
vegetables	0.30	cloves	26.
cranberries	0.30	tea leaves	28
blackstrap molasses	0.36	soil	85
rhubarb	0.40	seaweeds	120
green beans	0.45		

Roughly 9% is absorbed.

Iodine

Iodine can only do one thing for you: it can enter the thyroid gland and become part of the hormone thyroxin—but that's nothing to sneeze at. Thyroxin is somehow able to control the rate at which food is broken down into energy, the speed at which our body runs, how much gasoline we burn up—however you want to put it. Hyperthyroidism, basically a genetic condition, makes a person early-to-bed, early-to-rise, wake up instantly, constantly and exceedingly active, always feel his days are too long. All this is caused by over-production of that one hormone. The other side of the coin, hypothyroidism, also happens. But it's not genetic.

Too little iodine in the diet means too little thyroxin in the bloodstream. Victims of this have trouble getting up in the morning, are sluggish through the early part of the day, and are just getting started when everyone else is going to bed—the day is much too short. Such a person is generally lethargic, tends to put on weight and has trouble keeping warm.

All this has special implications for women because

thyroxin is necessary for the breakdown of estrogens. So too little thyroxin means too much estrogen. This in turn brings intense and poorly-timed menstrual periods, water retention, and a dangerously high tendency towards clotting. The problem is a common one and the solution is iodine.

It would be nice if all we had to do was eat right to get the iodine we need, but wide variations in soil's iodine content makes most food unreliable. The soil got that way because of rain, billions of gallons of it washing over the land through millions of years, washing the most soluble salts away into the rivers and down to the sea. Evaporation steals back a little iodine, which may fall into coastal soils as rain. So that's where our iodine is, in the ocean. And that's why fish and seaweed are the best food sources of this mineral. That's also why the ocean is so salty; it used to be no saltier than our blood.

Seeing as how fish and seaweed are not staple foods in this country, the government developed an alternate way to get iodine to its people—iodized salt. Of course not all salt is iodized, but the salt that is, says so. And, being 0.01% potassium iodide, a teaspoon should supply about 200 micrograms.

Another way to do your thyroid a favor is to eat thyroid. It's available on prescription, one brand name being Synthoid. Thyroxin itself is available too, as is the thing that iodine binds to to make thyroxin—thyroglobulin. Brand names for patented thyroxin concoctions include Choloxin, Euthoid and S-P-T. But save yourself some money. Get plain old thyroxin, which is in the public domain and therefore a lot cheaper. The same goes for thyroglobulin, one of whose brand names is Proloid.

It should be mentioned though, that some people are very

sensitive to these things. Give them a little thyroid and suddenly they're hyperthyroid cases. Also remember that, just as too little thyroxin makes clotting a possibility, too much can lead to hemorrhaging.

As if it weren't bad enough that food's got no iodine, some foods can ruin the iodine you get elsewhere. Those foods, including spinach, lettuce, cabbage, turnips, beets, and rutabagas, all contain something called thio-oxazidone which blocks iodine absorption. Luckily this stuff is inactivated by cooking.

Who can you trust when you can't trust nature?

Iodine (mg/100 gm)

water, oranges, and mushrooms	0.00020	cow's milk	0.0070
wine	0.00100	spinach	0.0090
whisky	0.0010	eggs	0.0090
grapefruit	0.0010	butter	0.0090
beer	0.0010	lard	0.0097
corn	0.0011	pig meat	0.0100
tomatoes	0.0012	lettuce	0.010
wheat	0.0012	cheeses	0.011
green peppers	0.0014	potatoes	0.015
oats	0.0015	pineapple	0.016
beets	0.0016	tea	0.016
honey	0.0018	soybeans	0.017
radishes	0.0018	liver	0.019
fruits	0.0020	cantaloupe	0.020
almonds	0.0020	peanuts	0.020
wheat germ	0.0020	vegetable oils	0.024
coconut	0.0020	crab	0.031
tuna	0.0023	halibut	0.046
veal	0.0028	turnip greens	0.047
alfalfa	0.0028	oysters	0.048
cashews	0.0030	herring	0.052
vegetables	0.0030	sunflower seeds	0.070
walnuts	0.0030	perch	0.074
freshwater fishes	0.0030	sea salt	0.095
lamb	0.0030	beans	0.100
apples	0.0030	lobster	0.10
salmon	0.0037	chard	0.10
coffee	0.0040	shrimp	0.13
medium molasses	0.0040	cod	0.14
grains	0.0040	haddock	0.31
cow meat	0.0060	soil	0.50
peaches	0.0060	cod liver oil	0.84
chicken	0.0060	iodized salt	
sea water	0.0060	(U.S.)	10
turkey	0.0060	seaweeds	62
cream	0.0060	kelp	180

Virtually all is absorbed.

Recommended Daily Allowances
for Iodine

	men	women
birth - 6 months	35 mcg	
6 months - 1 year	45	
1 - 3 years	60	
4 - 6 years	80	
7 - 10 years	110	
11 - 14 years	130	115
15 - 18 years	150	115
19 - 22 years	140	100
23 - 50 years	130	100
51+	110	80
pregnant women		125
lactating women		150

Copper

This essential mineral sometimes seems a greater danger when it is present than when it isn't. It's a vital building block of one of the cytochromes, though its main job is the controlled oxidation of vitamin C. Some of vitamin C's functions depend on its being oxidized in the process of doing them, including the breakdown of histamine. For all of them, a copper-containing enzyme is used to catalyze C's oxidation.

Copper also has a third duty, that of oxidatively tying up the loose ends in the structural proteins collagen and elastin, thus keeping them strong. Rats on copper-deficient diets developed little nicks in their aortas which soon began collecting cholesterol. Elastin is a major contituent of the aorta wall.

So copper is definitely a mineral worth having around and if you have reason to believe you're not getting enough, though it rarely happens, then by all means do something about it. But if you're going to take a supplement, *please* get one that's chelated. Inorganic copper can be pretty dangerous stuff, the symptoms of a mild dose being headache, nausea, and fatigue. And to get these, all you have to do is drink hot water that passed through a copper pipe or eat food cooked in a copper pan.

Copper (mg/100 gm)

sea water	0.00030	kale	0.30
water	0.00100	eggplant	0.30
sea salt	0.0047	bee pollen	0.32
tea	0.0100	rice	0.36
coffee	0.020	coconut	0.39
eggwhite	0.020	avocado	0.39
butter	0.030	tuna	0.50
vegetable oils	0.030	bananas	0.51
egg yolk	0.030	seaweeds	0.60
grapefruit	0.040	almonds	0.68
cantaloupe	0.040	barley	0.70
peaches	0.050	lentils	0.71
whisky	0.060	oats	0.74
eggs	0.070	ginseng	0.75
beer	0.070	cashews	0.76
cow meat	0.080	salmon	0.80
lettuce	0.090	kelp	0.80
pig meat	0.090	cloves	0.87
wine	0.100	walnuts	0.90
tomatoes	0.11	brazil nuts	1.1
soybeans	0.11	medium molasses	1.2
vegetables	0.12	hazelnuts	1.4
cheeses	0.14	honey	1.7
dill	0.14	soil	2.0
corn	0.15	black pepper	2.1
cow's milk	0.15	lobster	2.2
potatoes	0.16	blackstrap molasses	2.2
cream	0.17	thyme	2.4
turkey	0.18	wheat germ	2.9
halibut	0.19	mussels	3.2
raw milk	0.19	oysters	3.4
lamb	0.24	liver	3.7
chicken	0.28	mushrooms	6.0

Roughly 45% is absorbed.

Zinc

We know that zinc helps vitamin A so zinc deficiency ought to, and does, have some things in common with vitamin A deficiency. But we also know a couple dozen different enzymes require zinc to operate. So how come there's no such thing as a clear-cut zinc deficiency? Don't know, but there isn't (yet). The only clue is that healing processes greatly increase zinc requirements.

Zinc's toxicity, at least, is understood. It appears that copper and zinc share an intestinal absorption site, and large amounts of ingested zinc can shut copper out of the ball-game completely, thus causing copper deficiency. Large amounts of copper could presumably do the same to zinc.

High-protein foods (remember those twenty enzymes) are generally the best sources.

Zinc (mg/100 gm)

sea water	0.0010	almonds	1.5
water	0.0010	rice	1.5
sea salt	0.016	millet	1.5
greens	0.070	mangos	1.9
peaches	0.090	clams	2.0
wine	0.100	buckwheat	2.0
grapefruit	0.10	eggs	2.1
whisky	0.10	bleu cheese	2.2
cantaloupe	0.10	peas	2.3
beer	0.10	avocadoes	2.4
lettuce	0.10	beans	2.4
oranges	0.10	barley	2.7
apples	0.10	walnuts	2.8
fruits	0.12	turkey	2.8
cherries	0.15	beets	2.8
radishes	0.16	cow meat	3.0
squash	0.21	coconut	3.0
cauliflower	0.23	corn	3.1
tomatoes	0.24	wheat	3.2
pineapple	0.26	rye	3.4
bananas	0.28	pig meat	3.4
cream	0.30	seaweeds	3.5
butter	0.30	bone meal	3.6
eggwhite	0.30	oats	3.7
vegetable oils	0.32	brewer's yeast	3.9
vegetables	0.35	medium molasses	4.6
milk	0.40	cocoa	4.8
mushrooms	0.40	chicken	4.8
tuna	0.50	soil	5.0
carrots	0.50	lamb	5.4
lard	0.50	egg yolk	5.5
spinach	0.70	sunflower seeds	6.6
cabbage	0.80	soybeans	6.7
kale	0.82	liver	7.0
cheeses	0.90	maple syrup	7.5
honey	0.90	blackstrap molasses	8.3
parsley	0.90	torula yeast	9.9
halibut	1.00	sesame seeds	10.
cashews	1.0	wheat germ	14
bran	1.1	herring	110
turnips	1.2	oysters	160
salmon	1.4		

About 40% is absorbed.

Recommended Daily Allowances
for Zinc

birth - 6 months	3 mg
6 months - 1 year	5
1 - 10 years	10
11+	15
pregnant women	20
lactating women	25

Selenium

This element bears a close resemblance to sulfur. In fact, taken by itself, selenium would be mistaken for sulfur. Our misguided metabolism'd start substituting selenium in some important sulfur compounds and selenium would be nothing more than a nuisance. But that's not the case, thanks to vitamin E.

Vitamin E keeps selenium out of trouble. Together they form compounds that can do things neither could do alone. But E and selenium help each other do the same basic things that E could do alone, but not as well. As yet, selenium is known to have only one special job of its own: it's a vital constituant of the free-radical regulating enzyme glutathione peroxidase.

Selenium (mg/100 gm)			
sea water	0.000040	peanuts	0.038
apples	0.000500	alfalfa	0.038
cream	0.00050	rice	0.039
green beans	0.00060	seaweeds	0.043
sea salt	0.00064	liver	0.050
bananas	0.00100	fresh-water fishes	0.050
cow's milk	0.0012	salt-water fishes	0.053
human milk	0.0021	soybeans	0.054
carrots	0.0022	shellfish	0.060
beans	0.0030	tomatoes	0.060
torula yeast	0.0040	barley	0.062
cheeses	0.0080	beets	0.065
eggs	0.0100	chicken	0.070
brewer's yeast	0.011	onions	0.080
lentils	0.011	vegetable oils	0.100
oats	0.012	peas	0.12
grains	0.015	beans	0.12
egg yolk	0.018	wheat	0.13
rye	0.020	mushrooms	0.14
soil	0.020	cabbage	0.25
garlic	0.020	corn	0.40
meats	0.022		

60% is absorbed.

Chromium

Chromium appears to act in some mysterious way to control blood sugar, which raises some intriguing questions about a connection between diabetes and chromium deficiency. Chromium is part of an organic complex that performs some as-yet unknown function in helping insulin shovel sugar into cells. Similar properties are ascribed to both magnesium and manganese. Also, deficiencies of both magnesium and chromium (individually) are reported to cause atherosclerosis in animals. And a few connections have been made between high blood sugar and heart disease. Could chromium deficiency be a cause of so-called "maturity onset" diabetes? Hopefully time will cast further light on this fertile and important subject.

Meanwhile, ironically, table sugar has barely 10% of the chromium it had back in the sugar cane. Half a milligram per day should be pretty safe. And yes, there is such a thing as a chromium supplement.

Chromium (mg/100 gm)			
sea water	0.0000050	maple syrup	0.018
sea salt	0.0000800	grains	0.020
water	0.00018	nuts	0.020
milk	0.00100	butter	0.021
fruits	0.0020	parsley	0.021
carrots	0.0033	blackstrap	
corn	0.0050	molasses	0.022
lard	0.0070	chicken	0.026
cow meat	0.0090	honey	0.029
vegetable oils	0.0100	fruits	0.030
pig meat	0.010	vegetables	0.040
seafoods	0.011	corn oil	0.047
lamb	0.012	brewer's yeast	0.063
parsnips	0.013	seaweeds	0.130
tomatoes	0.014	cloves	0.15
meats	0.014	wheat	0.18
corn syrup	0.015	black pepper	0.37
rice	0.016	thyme	1.00
eggs	0.017	soil	10.

Less than 1% is absorbed.

Molybdenum

Molybdenum is incorporated into the structure of two enzymes, one of which is important and the other of which isn't that exciting. No one knows what happens when you get a molybdenum deficiency because it seems never to have happened.

How much a person should get in his daily ration is also a secret.

But we do know what happens when you get too much (however much that is); just like zinc, too much molybdenum induces a copper deficiency, which in turn causes a special kind of anemia.

It's surprising there's even this much to say about it.

Molybdenum (mg/100 gm)			
water	0.000035	wheat germ	0.056
sea water	0.0010	squash	0.065
seafoods	0.0010	gooseberries	0.068
milk	0.0020	wheat	0.079
haddock	0.0030	rye	0.090
tomatoes	0.0060	dill	0.110
wine	0.0065	liver	0.15
cow meat	0.0070	soil	0.20
fruits	0.0100	honey	0.20
eggwhite	0.012	pig meat	0.37
chicken	0.014	peas	0.60
sea salt	0.016	beans	0.70
raw milk	0.020	soybeans	1.10
blackstrap molasses	0.029	seaweeds	1.6
vegetables	0.050		

Roughly half is absorbed.

Vanadium

Vanadium (rhymes with stadium) is supposed to have something to do with regulating blood cholesterol, it's supposed to lower it.

Oils are a good source. Seafood is even better.

The human daily requirement, if there is any, can probably be measured in atoms.

Vanadium (mg/100 gm)			
cow's milk	0.0000010	ginseng	0.0023
apples	0.0000027	sea salt	0.0032
cauliflower	0.0000076	lobster	0.0043
tomatoes	0.0000078	radishes	0.0052
fruits	0.0000400	meats	0.0100
potatoes	0.000082	dill	0.014
water	0.000100	nuts	0.070
human milk	0.00018	parsley	0.079
sea water	0.00020	grains	0.110
calf's liver	0.00024	seafoods	0.17
mackerel	0.00026	vegetable oils	0.34
sardines	0.00090	seaweeds	0.53
lettuce	0.00210		

0.640% of eaten vanadium is absorbed.

So What?

After all this how much do we really know? We've identified a lot of important food factors but have we found
them all? Certainly not: there are literally millions of
things in food whose effects on health have never been
tested. But even when we've achieved full understanding of
nature and pioneered the food frontier, there remains the
possibility of out-engineering our bodies—designing parts
that surpass the heritage of evolution.

And why not? All vitamins are parts, pieces of molecular
machinery whose structure and composition completely determine their ability to do the job they do. Eventually,
when our understanding of the overall mechanism is suffi-
ciently complete, some genius will come up with a modifica-
tion in the vitamin that will improve that ability.

And this is not a science fiction suggestion, it's an in-
evitability. In fact it's already happened; remember that
vitamin K_3, a man-made molecule, is much more potent
than K_1, or K_2, the natural forms? Once science has tasted
success with a few of the parts it'll set its sights on bigger

game, and by the time this sort of thing really gets going technology might serve us up a spanking new, completely original, synthetic body. Then what will become of the science of nutrition when our bodies are powered by solar energy or nuclear fusion? Well that's for the people (or whatever you'd call them) of the future to worry about, so let's get back to the problems of today.

Our uncertainty as to how much of a vitamin the average guy should get is compounded by the fact that very few, if any, of us are average guys. Each person is genetically, and therefore biochemically, unique—since genes are nothing more than the blueprints for our biochemistry. Now throw in the fact that we are adaptable—different environments inhibiting or activating genes in different ways—and that no two people lead identical lives, even in the same environments, and you've got real chaos.

Faced with a problem like this about the best we can do is sort humans into two categories, depending on how active (generally) their stomach enzymes are. With relatively active enzymes, the stomach can extract energy from (oxidize) food very quickly; zipping right through the simple carbohydrates, laying into the more difficult proteins and even grind down the really tough guys—fats—all in a relatively short time. Such a person generally inclines toward salty foods when he's hungry because saltiness is characteristic (pretzels, saltines, etc. excluded) of rich, fatty foods. This guy can eat steak and eggs for breakfast and be hungry an hour later. Things like bread and potatoes don't interest him at all.

The other sort inclines towards sweets, towards light, starchy foods. A mayonnaise and avocado sandwich will sit in his stomach like a rock for hours. He should be careful not to overeat.

Fast oxidizers have to watch out for hypoglycemia while the slow ones are predisposed to diabetes (hyperglycemia).

But the point is that slow oxidizers have higher co-enzyme requirements: you might even say they have deficiencies. Maybe this could cause a vicious cycle—the deficiency causes one to burn food less efficiently, extract fewer vitamins, increase his deficiency, decrease his efficiency, etc. etc. etc. Or maybe the fast oxidizers should worry about those three or four hour stretches between meals. If he converts all his food to energy in an hour, and his cells gobble it all up in, say, another hour, then two hours after breakfast his blood sugar level is low and if he can't grab a bite he's in danger of insulin shock.

Does this mean that fast oxidizers are suffering from a vitamin surplus? Don't ask me. But it certainly means that the three-meals-a-day dogma is dangerously inflexible. This whole field is so new that your opinions on the subject are as good as anyone's, especially since no one knows better than you what you need.

Maybe your requirements for most vitamins are about average but your need for, say, thiamin is six times higher than the average. It's possible. If you feel something is wrong, by all means discuss it with a doctor. But the doctor's opinion—and I don't care who he is—is only an opinion. Ask three doctors and you'll get three different opinions. So make your *own* decision, based on what you feel.

Well, if doctors are not to be implicitly trusted on the subject of nutrition, the same is doubly true of vitamin manufacturers—which is four times as bad because we are doubly influenced by them. If you don't think so just close your eyes and see what the word "vitamin" brings to mind. . . . It's a god-damned pill!

Even when we know better it's difficult not to make that

kind of association. And it's not surprising, considering that the bulk of the information disseminated about vitamins comes from the people who make, and of course sell, vitamin products. The recent sales boom in this area has attracted mass marketing techniques that aim for a chain reaction of sales into subdivisions of the same thing. Now a description like that calls for an example.

A hundred years ago soap could be found in every home. If something—anything—was dirty, you cleaned it with soap. In those days, your soap manufacturer was guaranteed a good, steady living because everyone needed soap. But, since no one could improve on it, the field didn't produce many millionaires. And then came the proliferators. Pretty soon there was soap for Mom, soap for Dad, soap for junior, soap for your hair, soap for your hands, soap for your face, soap for the dishes, soap for the clothes, soap for the windows, soap for the floors, soap for the dog, soap for baby's hair. . . . and before you knew it the average guy felt inadequate without forty different kinds of soap in the house.

Now the same thing is happening with vitamins—vitamins for when you're overweight, vitamins for when your husband can't get an erection, vitamins for when you see a gray hair. . . .—and they won't be happy till you've built a new wing on your house to store them all. So how can we cope with all these miraculous new vitamins? Well first we have to understand the multivitamin, the granddaddy of them all.

The multivitamin is gonna give you everything. It's going to find out how much you need of every last vitamin and mineral, it's going to throw them all together with a little extra to make sure, and then jam all those vitamin complications into a convenient little pill. So now Joe Slick can coolly eat junk all day, turn the channel when they start talking about vitamins on TV and sadly shake his head when he sees people worrying themselves sick over nutrition—because he's got it made: he'll never get a vitamin deficiency because that one little pill he washes down with his morning coffee has got it all.

Well, forgetting that multivitamins ignore biochemical individuality, forgetting that most multivitamins omit nutrients that are known to be necessary and all of them omit nutrients that aren't yet known to be necessary, forgetting that most multivitamins have unbalanced proportions and all of them promote folic acid deficiency because of the FDA's very low ceiling on that vitamin, forgetting *all* that—those daily tablets are going to be a *terrible* drag on Joe's system. (Not that Joe's reading this of course, he takes multivitamins so that he won't have to read this.)

Most of the wonderful things that those pills supply more than enough of are things that have their own unique path of elimination from the body. Those paths of elimination usually involve a chain of enzymes that prepare the nutrient for the exodus. Now it's true that a few of those enzymes (a few percent) will be helped a very little by the vitamins the tablet supplies. But vitamins are only *co*-enzymes, not the enzyme itself, not nearly, they're tiny compared to the actual enzyme. And then most of the enzymes won't get any help at all, but they'll have a big job to look forward to each and every day, without relent. The accelerated wearing out of these enzymes will eventually tax the body's enzyme-making machinery to the breaking point. If Joe invests in a high-potency vitamin, so much the worse.

The multivitamin is the model for all the "specially tailored to your needs" concoctions. These usually start with a high potency multivitamin formula and then toss out the ingredients that don't seem to have anything to do with whatever the manufacturer is trying to do for you. Sometimes they don't even bother to do that.

As for the single-vitamin preparations, they're a little different. First, if you're really sick, drop this book and go see a doctor. If you're still with us and you happen to have one of the few conditions that can be linked with mild deficiencies of specific vitamins, then maybe vitamins can help you. One promising field of ongoing research is trying to relieve uncomfortable states of mind with the B vitamins. This field is not exactly new, but unambiguous results have been a long time coming and most of them still haven't arrived yet.

If you find your nerves chronically jangled, your mind confused and restless, and your sleep fitful and erratic, the vitamin to try is B_6. It doesn't take much, maybe 50 mg, and should be accompanied by magnesium, in the balanced form of dolomite.

Thiamin may help the opposite problem; having a ho-hum attitude, where everything looks the same and nothing seems to matter. Before you have time to get depressed, try B_1.

C is recommended when a trying experience leaves you feeling kind of weak and empty inside.

Dozens of other nutrients are available in the pure form and doubtless they each have unique mild deficiency symptoms; subtle signs that we notice but don't heed because we don't know how. Experience and educated guesswork will eventually tell us how, so keep your ears open to the experiences of others and your senses tuned to the goings-on of your own body. But the only way to find out if a particular vitamin will help *you* is to try it.

Now before you go and invite a mob of molecules into the

privacy of your insides you want to know something about them—so go back and read the appropriate chapter. Next, if you're still going through with it, select a relatively low dosage per tablet and don't get a whole lot of tablets. There are two reasons (besides spoilage) for this last.

First, don't *ever* develop pill-taking routines, your body hates them as much as your mind does. It craves variety. Even if you don't get *any* vitamins in your food your body hates to see that same old pill coming down the pipe every time; it gets bored sick of it. Better no pill at all.

And second, you have to remember that your mild deficiency arose from poor eating. Okay, if it's C it might be the same deficiency we've all got and if it's E, it might be something you picked up quite a while ago even if your eating is impeccable now. But otherwise you gotta start doing something about the way you eat.

If you try a vitamin for a little while and it doesn't work, stop taking it. If you have a deficiency in something else and you try going through the other fifty or so nutrients to find which it is, you could die first.

And if it does work then you know you had a deficiency and it wasn't a deficiency of vitamin pills, it was a deficiency of a certain kind of food and food is a lot more complicated than pills. That deficiency you got was just the first one in line; others are waiting to gang up on you. So you can't really treat anything with vitamin pills for long, and if you're not feeling as good as you know you could, it's only a matter of how long it's going to take you to do something about the way you eat.

Man can make jars of flawlessly translucent glass and pills with purity exceeding 0.0001%. He can coat them with any color of the rainbow. . . .

But only God can make a carrot.

Glossary

acetate-replacing factor: lipoic acid
adermin: pyridoxine
aneurin: thiamin
animal protein factor: cobalamin
antiberiberi factor: thiamin
antineuritic factor: thiamin
antirachitic vitamin: vitamin D
antiscorbutic vitamin: ascorbic acid
antisterility vitamin: alpha tocopherol
anti-stress factors: one or more compounds that seem to help the liver survive poisonings; found in most raw foods, especially liver and yeast
beriberi: terminal thiamin deficiency
bios IIB: biotin
cevitamic acid: ascorbic acid
coenzyme A: a chemical potholder, made in the body
coenzyme Q: ubiquinone$_{10}$
erythrotin: cobalamin
factor I: pyridoxine
factor X: used, at various times, in reference to cobala-

min, biotin, and alpha tocopherol

factor Y: pyridoxine

fermentation L: folic acid with three glutamates

hepatoflavin: riboflavin

heptoglutamate: folic acid with three glutamates

hexuronic acid: ascorbic acid

L. (for lactobacillus) casei factor: folic acid with three glutamates

laetrile: amygdalin

lyochrome: riboflavin

MDRs: minimum daily requirements, they're no longer in use

oryzamin: thiamin

ovoflavin: riboflavin

oxythiamin: a thiamin antagonist, it induces a thiamin deficiency

POF: lipoic acid (don't know what it stands for)

pellagra: terminal niacin deficiency

polyneuramin: thiamin

pteroylmonoglutamic acid: folic acid

pyrithiamin: a thiamin antagonist

RDAs: daily allowances of nutrients as recommended by the Food and Drug Administration, often a compromise between the nutritional needs of the American people and the financial desires of the food industry

rachitamin: vitamin D

rachitasterol: vitamin D

rickets: severe vitamin D deficiency when found in children, not usually fatal

scurvy: terminal ascorbid acid deficiency

thioctic acid: lipoic acid

ubiquinone: a coenzyme for electron transport, made by the body and found in animal foods; a plant compound, plastoquinone, can substitute for it

uroflavin: riboflavin

vitamin B: the B complex

vitamin B$_{12}$a, B$_{12}$b or d: cobalamin combined with water (aquocobalamin)

vitamin B$_{12}$c: nitritocobalamin

vitamin B$_\mu$:   a mixture of manganese and choline

vitamin B$_t$:   carnitine

vitamin F: thiamin; now used by some to designate the essential fatty acids

vitamin G: riboflavin

vitamin H: pyridoxine; also biotin

vitamin L$_1$:   helps rat mothers nurse; found in beef liver

vitamin L$_2$:   like L$_1$; found in yeast

vitamin PP: niacin

vitamin Q: rumored to help clotting; found in soy, but nobody knows what it is

vitamin U: metioninic acid

yeast eluate factor: pyridoxine

Index

199, 207-210
manganese 41-2, 217-8
meat 83
megaloblastic anemia 103
membranes 89
menopause 200
menstruation 196
mental retardation 78
mescalin 61
methionine 77, 101, 117
methotrexate 102
methyl groups 5, 47, 58, 60-2,
    100, 113-4, 117, 123
milk 158, 201
mineral oil 20
mitochondria 133
molybdenum 237
multivitamin 244-5
myelin 74
myoglobin 195

NAD 57-8
nerves 32-3, 40
nicotine 65
nicotinic acid 66
night blindness 12
nitrates 20
nitrites 16
nitrogen 193
noradrenalin 59

oleic acid 180, 183-4
orange juice 148-9
osteomalacia 156
oxalic acid 82

oxygen 99, 163-5, 181-2, 195

PABA 129-131
pancreas 79-80
pangamic acid 123-4
parathyroid glands 156
pellagra 56-7
pernicious anemia 90-1, 93-5,
    99, 103
peroxides 164, 181-2
phosphates 39-40, 47, 49, 57,
    84, 199
phosphorus 193, 199-201, 204-5
photons 50
phytic acid 128
pituitary gland 72
potassium 193, 211-4
pregnancy 81-2, 85, 103-4, 196
proline 136
propionic acid 90-1
prostacyclin 181-2
prostaglandins 15, 146-7, 181
protein 4-5, 21
protons 192
psoriasis 15
psilocybin 60
psychedelics 60-1, 64

red cells 99-100
retinol 11-24
rheumatic fever 165-6, 168
riboflavin 47-53, 65
rickets 156
RNA 15
rutin 177